Fr. John Porta
that an ordinary person can incorporate into his
day-to-day life, using words of saints and spiritual
authors. If you are looking for one book that will
explain each of these spiritual activities that you
can try to insert in your busy schedule, grab a copy!

Oliver M. Tuazon
Author, *No Holds Barred:*
Questions Young People Ask

I had the privilege of meeting the author, Fr. John
Portavella, in Chicago some 50 years ago, when I was
on my way home from graduate studies at Harvard.
At that time, Fr. John was serving as chaplain of a
center of Opus Dei catering to students and professionals. He has been serving in that capacity since
then, and mostly in the Philippines.

Fr. John has spent many hours listening to
people who, in many instances, have come to him
for spiritual direction. I am very happy that he has
decided to write this book, which puts together his
perspectives gained from many years of giving practical spiritual advice to Filipinos. His perspectives
are rich; they are of great use to people of any age
and of any place, who are open to coming closer to
God, as well as bringing their friends closer to God.

This book is addressed to men and women who
are out in the middle of the world living their own
life and doing their work within a profession of their
choice. It is intended for those still young enough to
be preparing for work as a professional; for actively
serving professionals; and for those who have
already gone through a lifetime of work and have
thus retired from full-time professional duties. It is

a treatise based on the actual experience of thousands of people on how to strike a proper balance between life and work in a unity of life, put together by the realization that we are children of God who calls us to do our best even as we go through the ordinary duties of our everyday life.

This book is a call to faith and joy, to operative faith, i.e., faith that is brought down to imbue every facet of life; a faith that takes care of details, because it is in the details that we find God waiting for us and ready to embrace us. It is a call to joy, because we may have failures and proofs of sinfulness but as we have been reminded, our Father God takes enormous pleasure in a child who fails and yet keeps trying, and in a sinner who goes back to Him asking for His pardon and blessing.

I consider this book a "must" read for ordinary men and women of any age, who grapple with the age-old questions: Where I am, and doing what I do, how can I get closer to my Father God? And how can I bring others with me so they too can get closer to our Father?

We owe Fr. John Portavella a vote of thanks for reflecting on his experiences in giving spiritual direction to thousands of people, and for putting together the key perspectives derived from such a rich and fruitful apostolate as his.

Jesus P. Estanislao, Ph.D.
Former Secretary of Finance
under President Cory Aquino
September 2013

Readers of *The Journey of Life* embark on an extraordinary discovery of the "radical love of God" and His divine gift of faith to those who seek, find, love, and serve Him. Based on exhaustive research and vast pastoral experience, Fr. Portavella presents clear evidence of how God discloses Himself, and how mankind fulfills an aspiration, a longing, and a destiny when united with Him.

Bombarded by scientific empiricism, materialism, and secularism that cloud or distract from the divine adventure of searching for the Great Unknown, the author inspires a leap of faith, hope, and love towards the Unveiled.

Esther Joos Esteban
Author, *The Work of Children*

Planning the
Journey of Life

John C. Portavella

Revised Edition

LEONINE PUBLISHERS
PHOENIX, ARIZONA

NIHIL OBSTAT
    Rev. Fr. Mark Emman H. Sese
    Censor
    Diocese of Pasig, Philippines

IMPRIMATUR
    ✠ Most Rev. Mylo Hubert C. Vergara, D.D.
    Bishop of Pasig, Philippines

Published by Leonine Publishers LLC
Phoenix, Arizona
USA

ISBN-13: 978-1-942190-31-8

Library of Congress Control Number: 2017935103

10 9 8 7 6 5 4 3 2 1

Visit us online at www.leoninepublishers.com
For more information: info@leoninepublishers.com

This book is dedicated to
Saint Josemaría Escrivá,
Blessed Alvaro del Portillo,
and *Bishop Javier Echevarría,*
as a token of gratitude, for their loving
paternity in successive periods of time.

It is also dedicated to my parents,
José María Portavella
and *María Casanova,*
who, with awesome faith and
stoutheartedness,
gladly made it possible.

Acknowledgements

I wish to express my heartfelt gratitude to all those who, in different ways, have contributed to the making of this book.

I will not attempt, here, to give due credit nominally to every one of them. I am sure though that God has known perfectly their efforts and will not fail to reward them very well.

Nonetheless, I think I have to make an exception with Jose Maria Mariano, Ph.D., President of the University of Asia and the Pacific, under whose auspices this book comes to light, and the late Col. Eduardo Ungson, Mr. Antonio Jon, Mr. Walter Brown, V. Pacquing Junt, and Mr. Wilson Ledesma, who also contributed to make this project a reality.

May the hidden God repay all of them a hundredfold.

Contents

Foreword

I first met the author of this book, Father John C. Portavella, way back in 1972 when I was taking care of a very small parish in Lipa, Batangas. We subsequently followed separate paths as he moved to the Visayan region in the south of the Philippines to carry out his apostolic tasks in Opus Dei. Throughout the years, however, we have maintained bonds of affection, prayer, priestly brotherhood, and fond memories.

Thus, I am very happy to offer this foreword to both his works on topics of universal interest: *The Hidden God* and *The Journey of Life*.

"*Truly you are a God Who hides Himself,*" we read in Isaiah 45:15. It might appear as a puzzling reality that the Almighty would be a silent and hidden witness to the most diverse happenings in the world and in our lives, of great accomplishments and of terrible events. On occasion, we might be tempted to wonder why God does not intervene more openly in order to advance a good cause, or to put an end to an evil one. It is what Benedict XVI referred to when he wrote, "*One can still ask why God did not make a world in which His presence is more evident—why Christ did not leave the world with another sign of His presence so radiant that no one could resist it. This is the mystery of God and man which we find so inscrutable.*"[1]

Without pretending to explain or fully decipher what will always remain a mysterious matter, the

---

[1] Benedict XVI, *Jesus of Nazareth* (New York: Doubleday, 2007), 34.

author presents a number of valuable insights into this intriguing question. After describing our current earthly situation and our very deep longing to see God, which are so vividly expressed in many of the Psalms, he describes our life as being, fundamentally, a test of faith. This latter assumption throws abundant light on why the Lord does not normally manifest Himself to us in an open and pellucid manner; and, in summarizing this discourse, the author emphatically states that, *this life is for faith, while the next Life is for vision.*

In a striking and quite original fashion, Fr. Portavella also views our life as a game played by the hidden God with each one of us, and he mentions some of the unwritten rules governing this game.

After considering the ways God frequently uses while dealing with us, the author points out the pivotal roles played by faith and human freedom in our earthly sojourn. **In the last part of the book, he offers the reader some conclusions, as well as practical suggestions flowing from the previously stated considerations which make this book very recommendable to a wide range of readers.** Finally, I am happy that this work comes to light during the Year of Faith, for it could definitely strengthen and revive the faith of many people.

+ GAUDENCIO B. CARDINAL ROSALES
Archbishop Emeritus of Manila

Introduction

"I am the Way."
John 14:6

hough hidden, God is a loving Father who follows every act we do in our lives with utmost interest. A few of our actions are important and consequential according to human standards. Most of them, however, are not. They are ordinary, prosaic, may be monotonous and even boring. And yet, they are potentially very great and truly significant for receiving eternal life. But in order to achieve that, we have to learn to transform these actions into an offering to God, our secluded Father.

When Jesus Christ, the visible image of the invisible God, came to this earth more than twenty centuries ago, He not only redeemed us and regained for us the condition of being loved as adopted sons of God, He also taught us the way to transform ordinary things and events in our lives into opportunities to please the Triune God, the hidden Examiner of our endeavors.

When our Lord came to this world, He did not work extraordinary feats, except for the episode in the temple when He was twelve years old.[1] Most of the time, His life did not differ very much from our own. He acted with naturalness, which corresponds to His condition as "perfect man," and He liked to refer to Himself as "the son of man."

----

[1] Lk 2:41-50.

1

If we want to give ordinary things a supernatural value, we have the perfect model in Jesus Christ. He not only redeemed us in His passion and death on Mount Calvary, but in all His actions, including the most seemingly unimportant ones.

In a similar manner, we are called to co-redeem with our Lord in all the moments and varying circumstances of our lives. For that, however, we need to unite ourselves to Jesus Christ, and through Him, with Him, and in Him, to do the will of God the Father, with the help of the Holy Spirit. In this way, we can become an everlasting gift to the Almighty.

In order to make such a lofty ideal a reality, we need to take concrete steps that will lead us to that high goal. This book attempts to achieve this aim by offering a number of suggestions that might be of help. Practically all of them came from St. Josemaría Escrivá de Balaguer, with whom this author had the blessed fortune to reside with in Rome during the period of September of 1955 to June of 1958.

In line with St. Josemaría's great love for freedom, it is important to emphasize that each one must feel completely free to adopt these suggested practices or follow different ways for his or her personal, spiritual journey. They are only suggestions which could help some people reach the goal of holiness, which is union with God. That is, to make an epic poem out of ordinary life. Nonetheless, it has to be said that these practices have immensely helped a great number of people from different walks of life in their quest to achieve union with God in the midst of the most ordinary circumstances of life.

Furthermore, these steps are not to be practiced all at once, but step by step, in a way recommended by a prudent spiritual director.

If we have searched for the hidden God, and found Him, and more so if we have had the great fortune of discovering Him as revealed in the person of Jesus Christ and His teachings as authoritatively expounded by the only Church He founded, the Roman Catholic Church, we will have a loving relationship with Him and will help others do the same.

Meanwhile, as we take the test of this life, God continues to be concealed in shadows. This book hopes to be an aid in this relationship with the secluded Lover.

St. Josemaría puts it lucidly, saying, *"May you seek Christ, may you find Christ, may you love Christ!"*

Planning the Journey of Life

One of the most prized gifts that God has given us is the gift of time. It is precious, for we only have one life to live which is limited, and our eternal lot depends on how we use it. It stands to reason, therefore, that we are to plan its use well. This is why we should make a plan on how to fulfill our obligations towards God, our family, our work commitments, our civic duties, and our personal interests, including our rest.

St. Josemaría states categorically: "If you don't have a plan of life, you'll never have order."[1] And he adds: "Virtue without order? Strange virtue!"[2]

Prof. Martin Rhonheimer writes:

> The plan of life adapts flexibly to each one's life. It does not add a spiritual structure parallel to ordinary life, but forms a unity with daily normalcy, until it is made into an encounter with God. The plan of life is the concrete and effective primary means to achieve a deep unity of life: unity between work and prayer, between ordinary life and dealings with God . . . . To faithfully fulfill the plan of life fosters in us the awareness of the nearness of God, and puts us under a permanent "tension" or apostolic "vibration" . . . . The Norms are fixed points, concrete things

---

[1] Josemaría Escrivá, *The Way* (Sinag-tala Publishers, 1985), no. 76.

[2] Ibid., no. 79.

5

that we resolve to fulfill with constancy and with certain discipline. They are like stone markers or kilometer posts that point out the way, and whose usefulness is shown precisely when there seem to be thousands of human reasons to delay or neglect dealing with God: tiredness, lack of time, excessive work, family problems, urgent tasks, etc.[3]

The effort to fulfill these practices of piety is by far compensated by the advantages derived from it. The words of our Lord apply very well to this case: "My yoke is sweet and my burden light."[4]

The Norms of piety are not to be viewed as mere *means*. Their goal, which is much more important, is union with God. St. Josemaría referred to the Norms when he wrote:

> The truth is, you tell me, "that it's not necessary for me to be a hero or to go to ridiculous extremes in order to persevere when I am forced to be isolated."
>
> And you add, "As long as I fulfill the 'norms' you gave me, I won't worry about the snares and pitfalls of my environment; to fear such trifles—that is what I would be afraid of." Wonderful![5]

Urban and modern life takes a fast pace or a rapid tempo. We will only succeed in avoiding being dragged by it if we have a commensurate inner spiritual rhythm given by the Norms of piety. It is not a

---

[3] Martin Rhonheimer, *You are the Light of the World* (Manila: Sinag-tala Publishers, 2010), 202.
[4] Mt 11:30.
[5] *The Way*, no. 986.

matter of reciting prayers fast for the sake of reciting them, but to truly love God.

We need *"to deal"* with Jesus Christ in friendly terms when doing the Norms of piety in our professional work, in our civic and social life, and also in our rest or playing sports. The life of Christ in us, in our souls, is our strength, our consolation, and our happiness.

But our soul, like our body, needs to be nourished. Similarly, in order to keep ourselves spiritually healthy, we need to accomplish the Norms of piety faithfully, so much so that we should feel bad for having missed a Norm of piety in a similar way as we would feel bad for having skipped a meal for some reason.

If we do so, they become a sure path of contemplative life and sanctity. As St. Josemaría would say, they turn out to be like those tall, red poles that, in very cold countries, are placed along paths that from time to time are covered with snow. As long as these signs are taken into account, none is in danger of falling into a ravine or perishing. And he adds:

> And how shall I acquire "our formation" and how shall I keep "our spirit?" By fulfilling the specific "norms" that your Director gave you, and explained to you, and made you love. Be faithful to them and you'll be an apostle.[6]

The management of time is very important. We need a *plan of life*, a well-thought-out timetable in which there is room for all our duties: To God, to family, to our work, and to our rest.

---

[6] Ibid., no. 377.

Friendship with God, says Antonio María Ramírez, a noted Spanish author, is sanctity.

> The saints are the friends of God. Sanctity is not the task of geniuses. We can all participate in the divine friendship; we can all know and love Jesus. It is a life-time project that, thanks to the divine Goodness, is within the reach of all who know how to love. It is a great love, indeed, that could appear to us as being beyond our capabilities. But He is the Way, the Truth and the Life . . . . I invite you to follow, in an orderly manner and little by little, an accessible plan of life that could be adapted to any family or professional situation; and by it you would endeavor to become more useful to God and to others. They are not new things; they are practices that have made saints out of many women and men. They are practices of piety that have sowed human history with peace and joy. They require a commitment to demand from oneself a bit more every day. They need constancy and, at the same time, humility and good humor. It is a commitment to love God who loves us very much and who is always waiting for something more, even if it is only a few words like "I love you," in the midst of our work.[7]

Andres Vazquez de Prada also wrote:

> St. Josemaría taught self-surrender [to God] takes place when the norms are lived; when

---

[7] Antonio María Ramírez, *Comprometerse* (Madrid: Ediciones Palabra, 2007), 14.

we cultivate a robust piety, including daily mortification and penance; when we try not to lose the habit of professional work and study; when we are eager to understand the spirit of our apostolate better every day; when discretion (not mysteriousness nor secretiveness) accompanies our work. And, above all, when we are continually conscious of being united in a special communion of saints, with all those who form part of our supernatural family.[8]

Some are afraid of committing themselves to a plan of life. They mistakenly think that it would rob them of freedom, but it is not the case.

The same author says,

A life of piety will help us to be free from adoring pagan gods: money, luxury, and success among others. A life of love of God, will help us to be free from selfishness, and thus to truly love others, without expecting anything in return. God will free us from prejudices and will lead us to seek, to find and to love the truth and its consequences.[9]

These practices of piety act as "catalytic" agents. This word, coined by Berzelius in 1836, is used to describe chemical reactions which are accelerated by a substance (the catalyst) which is not changed in the process. A small amount of catalyst can produce the conversion of a large amount of the substance being changed. In our spiritual life, something very

---

[8] Andres Vazquez de Prada, *The Founder of Opus Dei*, vol. 2 (New York: Scepter Publishers Inc., 2003), 249.

[9] Ibid., p. 16.

similar happens, and the Norms of piety act as catalysts. They could also be compared to an oxygen tank that allows us to move safely in the midst of all the different environments, even when the air is polluted.

The proper fulfillment of the Norms of piety is something that demands faith. To give priority to these spiritual practices in an ordinary busy day of work requires belief in the veiled God. He is our Father, He is watching us all the time, and deserves that we do not take Him as "second best." The Norms of piety are to come first in our list of priorities; the reason being that they directly pertain to the glory of God. Here applies very well the universally recognized motto: *"First things first!"* Consequently, the axiom, *"The Norms come first!"* becomes a fitting principle to adopt to guide us in our often-busy lives. For their performance, we are to reserve our best time and place, never what is left over; God deserves it so. They are to be the first in our timetable, as well as in our mind (hierarchy of values) and in our heart (hierarchy of love). The reason for this is that they provide the connecting supernatural thread that unites all the diverse aspects of our life. Each one is meant to be a loving encounter with Christ, and they are there to help us become connected and transformed into Him.

These freely-adopted practices are never to be taken as if they were "unwanted visitors" that we entertain grudgingly. On the contrary, we are to love doing them, for each one is a personal and intimate encounter with the great Love of our lives.

We are to be faithful to the Norms of piety. This is particularly true when we find ourselves spiritually weak; it is the time when we most need to rely on these practices of piety. All of them are important and they form a single compact whole.

These practices of piety should not be abandoned just because we feel dry and without enthusiasm. St. Josemaría explained it lucidly:

> If the thought ever passes through our minds, in the face of effort or dryness that we are "play-acting," our reaction should be to think that the wonderful moment has come to perform a human play for a divine spectator. God is the spectator: the Father, the Son, and the Holy Spirit: the blessed Trinity. And together with God our Lord, the Mother of God and the angels and saints will also be watching us.
>
> We cannot abandon our life of piety, our life of sacrifice and love. When we act out a play for God, for love of Him, trying to please Him; when we "go against the grain"; when we feel we are playing the role of a jester; let us think that we are jesters of God.[10]

It stands to reason that we should be careful not to "pile the Norms up" in the last minutes of the day. If we do so, we run the risk of converting the last portion of the day into something that resembles a "holy hour," which is good in itself, but certainly not the best for a sound and normal family life.

Work and the Norms of piety are not to be viewed as separate realities. In fact, if we pray much, we will do our work well. St. Josemaría explained it this way:

[10] Josemaría Escrivá, *Letter*, March 24, 1931, 18-19.

We do not lead a double life, but a unity of life, which is simple and strong and in which all our actions are united.

When we respond generously to this spirit, we acquire a second nature. Without realizing it, we are thinking of our Lord all day long, and we feel an impulse to put God into everything, for without Him, nothing would have any attraction. The time then comes when we can't tell where prayer ends and where work begins; for our work is also prayer, contemplation, a true life of mystical union with God without oddities. This is "good divinization."[11]

There should not be piety without work, nor work without piety.

As for the proper priorities, the following anecdote is very telling: In 1997, in Argentina, Bishop Javier Echevarría was asked something like this: "Father, how can I do all the Norms, considering that I am very busy in my profession?" The answer was quick: "Let us invert this. The question should be: 'How can I do my work, after doing all my Norms?'"

Therefore, our guiding principle should never be, "What do I like to do now?" or "What do I feel like doing now?" but rather, "What do I ought to do now?" or its equivalent, "What is it that God wants me to do in this very moment?"

To the question on how to overcome the tension between the Norms of piety and professional work, the prelate of Opus Dei replied: "We should not

----

11 Ibid., May 6, 1945.

separate these realities. We do our work well if we pray much."

These practices of piety adapt themselves to the most varied sets of circumstances. They are not rigid structures, but rather, flexible programs of life that fit in our daily schedules "like a rubber glove fits into the hands of a surgeon," as St. Josemaría was fond of saying. On occasion, there might be unforeseen events; we have to be ready to change plans. In most cases, it will be better to advance the fulfillment of a Norm than to postpone it.

Moreover, our duties towards our relatives, our family, should never be sacrificed on the altar of our professional work. It is a case of what can be called a "professionalitis," a kind of "sickness" by which a person exaggerates his or her focus on the demands of work, at the expense of other equally or more important concerns. The care for the family God has given us is the most important "business" that we have in our hands (as St. Josemaría was also fond of saying). Hence, it would be wrong to spend so much time in the office doing overtime, or being so immersed in professional work that there is hardly any time left for the family. It would lead to disorder, a serious one, that would displease our Lord.

Similarly, our social and civic duties should not be neglected with the excuse that we are "too busy." Helping to foster the common good, each according to his or her position and role, is an "obligation. . . inherent in the dignity of the human person."[12] "No one can allow himself to wallow in the luxury of a

---

[12] *Catechism of the Catholic Church*, no. 1913.

merely individualistic morality."[13] Thus, for instance, it is the mind of the Church that, "as far as possible, citizens should take an active part in public life."[14]

Finally, our own personal health, recreation, and rest are not to be neglected either. We are only stewards of our physical endowments, and God expects us to take good care of them for Him. In consequence, we are to see to it that we eat healthy food with a balanced diet, sleep enough to recover our energy, exercise sufficiently, and have regular medical check-ups. In addition, we are to avoid whatever could undermine our health, such as excessive drinking of alcoholic beverages or smoking.

At this point, with the above ideas in mind, let us consider how an ordinary day could be like.

The First Battle

A new day begins. The alarm clock sounds. It is time to get up quickly from bed. The moment has arrived to offer the first sacrifice to our Lord. The body says, "No, not yet!" but the soul says, "Yes! It is time!" And the most important part, the soul, must conquer. It is the first of the many affirmations of love that, with His help, are to come throughout the day. It is not a matter of thinking that we are better than others, but to struggle with oneself, being aware that the sweetest victory is over oneself, and when it is offered to God.

---

[13] Pope Paul VI, Pastoral Constitution *Gaudium et Spes*, Dec. 7, 1965, no. 30.
[14] *Catechism of the Catholic Church*, no. 1915.

"'The heroic minute.' It is time to get up, on the dot! Without hesitation, a supernatural thought and . . . up! The heroic minute; here you have a mortification that strengthens your will and does not weaken your body."[15] St. Josemaría further explains the reason for this practice:

> Conquer yourself each day from the very first moment, getting up on the dot, at a set time, without granting a single minute to laziness. If, with the help of God, you conquer yourself in that moment, you'll have accomplished a great deal for the rest of the day.
>
> It's so discouraging to find yourself beaten in the first skirmish![16]

St. Mark tells us, "In the morning, a great while before day, He [Jesus] rose and went out to a lonely place, and there He prayed."[17] It is in this fashion that our Lord has taught us how to begin the day aright.

It is time to become agile and set sluggishness aside. It is a good moment to say, *"I shall serve!"* in daring response to Satan's suggestion: *"I will not serve!"* Together with these first offerings, there could be the first prayer addressed to the entire *"Company of veiled Spectators."* First among them is the Triune God, to Whom we will offer our entire day, each one of us in his or her fashion. Since the morning offering is something very personal, each one has his or her own way of making it. Perhaps we

---

15 *The Way*, no. 206.
16 Ibid., no. 191.
17 Mk 1:35.

could say, like St. Josemaría: "All my thoughts, all my words, all the actions of this day, I offer to You, Lord, and all out of Love."[18] It makes much sense that the first thought and the first act of love would be for the concealed Lover who is constantly seeking our attention. It will be a big boost to our attempts to be with the Lord throughout the day.

It is the moment to greet our Lord and thank Him for the gift of a new day. We offer Him all our actions and our entire life. It is moving to think of the many generations of Christians that have passed on the wonderful custom of offering to God all the actions of the day, from the parents to their children. The morning offering gives meaning and purpose to our whole day. It starts our conversation with the veiled Lord. It is important to offer our work to God, for otherwise we are only doing it for some other goal. For example, for the money we get, for the prestige it brings us, etc.

The purpose of the morning offering is to dedicate every action of the day to God. And every action, except sin, can be offered to Him. St. Paul says, "Whether you eat or drink or whatever else you do, do all for the glory of God."[19] With this act, all our activities for the day are dedicated to the Lord through a virtual intention acceptable to Him. If this intention is renewed in other moments of the day, it would be so much better.

The consciousness that our day has been offered to the veiled Lord is a great help in performing well in our daily struggle. Before the famous Battle

---

[18] *"Todos mis pensamientos, todas mis palabras, las obras todas de este día, te ofrezco, Señor, y todo por Amor."*
[19] 1 Cor 10:31.

of Trafalgar, Admiral Nelson simply said: "England expects that every man will do his duty."[20] The British soldiers were motivated, for they knew why they were fighting. The morning offering reminds us of the purpose of our daily actions and of the King we serve.

After this, it is a good moment to address Our Lady (maybe kissing the scapular of Our Lady of Carmel) and St. Joseph, our Guardian Angel, the saints, as well as the souls in Purgatory, and to formulate the desire of gaining all the indulgences that our loving Mother, the Church, has granted to us for the day that is beginning.

In a childlike manner (provided we are certain nobody sees us doing it, for they would not understand what we were doing), we might want to wave at them, and perhaps focus our attention on someone from that great multitude of witnesses: a saint of our devotion, a relative, or a friend who has already passed away. This contact with the other world is very comforting. If we were to hesitate and think that such a practice would be childish, we only need to remember that our Lord said, "Whoever does not receive the kingdom of heaven like a child shall not enter it."[21]

If medically permitted, that is, if there is no contraindication, entering the cold shower without delay early in the morning could be an excellent sacrifice to offer to the unseen Lord. It is an opportunity to communicate with Him, thus supernaturalizing this daily hygienic practice. Moreover, it is

---

[20] Royal Museums Greenwich, http://www.rmg.co.uk.
[21] Lk 18:17.

also an excellent way to drive away possible temptations that may occur at this time.

Surely, to be aware that we are surrounded by a whole "Company of Witnesses" is an effective way of avoiding sin, as well as of feeling well accompanied. The daily "rituals" we perform routinely, like dressing and getting ready for the day could be given much worth and meaning if we attach a multitude of spiritual interactions or aspirations to them. Simply put, by praying. For example, we can imitate St. Josemaría who, upon fastening the buttons on his clothing, used to say something like, "Jesus, fasten me to You!"

Physical exercise, like calisthenics, is another good chance to convert a possibly tedious experience into a spiritually uplifting one.

The trip to a nearby church lends itself to a period of inner and exterior silence with the recollection that the traffic situation allows. While fastening the buckle of the seat belt, it is a good moment to invoke the Guardian Angel, who is one of those "unseen witnesses," and who is ever ready to help us. Afterwards, the blessing for a trip recommended by St. Josemaría comes in handy: "Through the intercession of the Blessed Mary, may I have a good trip. May the Lord be in my journey; and may His Angel accompany me!"

A red light at the intersection might be a challenge for our patience. Use this time as an opportunity to react supernaturally, perhaps saying to our Lord: "Most Sacred Heart of Jesus, give us peace!" And at a green light: "Holy Mary, our Hope, pray for us!"

The First Appointment

We have now reached the church. The time for intense communication with the supernatural world has arrived. If we have not done so in the house, some minutes of mental prayer will serve well as preparation for the Holy Mass. And if we feel that we do not have the time for it, for we have a lot of pending things, then, *we make time* for prayer: "First things first!" An intense period of contact with God in our daily periods of prayer will lead us to find Him in the ordinary activities in which we engage.

> We children of God have to be contemplatives: people who, in the midst of the din of the throng, know how to find silence of soul in a lasting conversation with our Lord, people who know how to look at Him as they look at a Father, as they look at a Friend, as they look at someone with whom they are madly in love.[22]

As much as possible, we are to say our prayers at a fixed time and with the help of a good book. If we do it in the office, we can tell the secretary to block that particular period, for we are "in conference." No visitors, no phone calls. We are communicating with God who is always ready to talk with us. We do not need to ask for an audience or to make

---

[22] Cf. Josemaría Escrivá, *The Forge* (Manila: Sinag-tala Publishers, 2000), no. 728.

an appointment beforehand. He is always listening, because He loves us infinitely.

It is a matter of conversing with the distinct Persons of the Blessed Trinity, with Our Lady or with anyone in the "Company of Witnesses" which constitutes our splendid family.

What is important is to fall in love with the Lord, to deal with Him, to do things that increase our friendship with the Triune God, and to avoid firmly whatever hurts this relationship. For that, the introductory prayer recommended by the founder of Opus Dei is very helpful:

> My Lord and my God, I firmly believe that you are here, that you see me, that you hear me. I adore you with profound reverence; I beg your pardon for my sins and the grace to spend this time of prayer fruitfully. My immaculate Mother, St. Joseph my father and lord, my guardian angel, intercede for me.

Notice that, in this prayer, we remind ourselves of the astonishing fact that God is here! That He, the Almighty, sees and hears us perfectly, although we, who are taking the great Test of our lives—a test on faith, hope, and love—do not. The situation is very similar to a one-way mirror. He sees us perfectly, but we do not see Him at all.

Observe also that after having expressed our deep respect for Him, we ask pardon for our sins. Our Lord does not listen to us merely because we are very good and behave very well, but because He loves us boundlessly. His love is so immense, that even if we had committed the greatest imaginable crimes, He is so merciful that He would still listen to us, provided that we were truly repentant of our sins.

St. Josemaría writes, "However unworthy the person, however imperfect the prayer turns out to be, if it is offered with humility and perseverance, God always hears it."[23] And he also wrote:

If we were to love ourselves excessively, then there would be every reason to be sad, on seeing all our failures and meanness. Such wretchedness might well sadden and discourage us. But if we love God above all things, and if we love others, and ourselves, in God and for God, then we have great reason for rejoicing! . . . . If ever you feel crestfallen on experiencing your own wretchedness, perhaps in a particularly vivid way, then, it is the moment to be completely docile and abandon yourself totally into God's hands. There is the story of a beggar who came up to Alexander the Great and asked him for alms. Alexander stopped, and commanded the man to be made ruler over five cities. The poor man, overwhelmed and bewildered, exclaimed: "But I did not ask for so much!" And Alexander replied: "You asked according to what you are; I am giving according to what I am."[24]

Thus, in the throes of His crucifixion, Jesus answered: "Truly I say to you today you will be with

---

[23] Josemaría Escrivá, *Furrow* (Manila: Sinag-tala Publishers, 2000), no. 468.
[24] Escrivá, *Letter*, March 24, 1931, 24-26.

me in Paradise," to a criminal who had told Him: "Remember me in your Kingdom!"[25] He did not reply, as we might have expected, with words such as, "I am the Holy of Holies; I do not talk to people like you!"

Once we have sincerely said, "I beg Your pardon for my sins," we must be convinced that we are forgiven, and that the concealed Father is listening with great affection to whatever we might say. Let us not doubt it. He is that merciful.

In the recommended introductory prayer, we also asked that we spend the time of prayer fruit-fully. This means that we wish to come out of it more united to the Almighty, more resolved to fulfill His will, as perhaps manifested in some specific resolutions. We wish to become more eager to serve others and help them to be happier by discovering our King and His *entourage* of angels, saints, and souls in Purgatory, paying court to the Lord. It does not necessarily mean that we have had an enjoyable time, but rather that God was pleased. We might have to struggle with distractions and experience spiritual dryness, but the Lord was pleased in seeing us persevering in our efforts.

As for the content of this friendly conversation with the unseen Lover, the advice of St. Josemaría is as ever clear and helpful:

> You wrote to me, "To pray is to talk with God. But about what?" About what? About Him, and yourself: joys, sorrows, successes and failures, great ambitions, daily worries—even your weaknesses! And acts of thanksgiving

---

25 Lk 23:42.

and petitions and love and reparation. In short, to get to know Him and to get to know yourself—get acquainted![26]

As if wanting to emphasize the importance of the awareness of God's presence in genuine prayer, St. Josemaría elaborates: "You don't know how to pray? Put yourself in the presence of God, and as soon as you have said, 'Lord, I don't know how to pray!' you can be sure that you have already begun."[27] He adds:

Mental prayer is this heart-to-heart dialogue with God in which the whole soul takes part; intelligence, imagination, memory and will are all involved. It is a meditation that helps to give supernatural value to our poor human life, with all its normal, everyday occurrences.[28]

And as to summarize what this kind of prayer is all about, he writes:

Do you remember? You and I were praying silently as night was falling. From close by came the murmur of water. And, through the stillness of the city, we also seemed to hear voices of people from many lands, crying to us in anguish that they do not yet know Christ. Unashamedly you kissed your Crucifix and you asked him to make you an apostle of apostles.[29]

---

[26] *The Way*, no. 91.
[27] Ibid., no. 90.
[28] St. Josemaría Escrivá, *Christ is Passing By* (Manila: Sinagtala Publishers, 1973, 2000).
[29] *The Way*, no. 811.

At prayer time, it is useful to bring with us some spiritual book, just in case we would need this material as we praise our Lord, express our love and dependence on Him, give thanks for so many blessings we have received, ask pardon for so many offenses and omissions we see upon examining our lives, and ask for things we and our relatives and friends need. If a particular passage of the book does not impress us particularly, all we have to do is to go on; perhaps another paragraph will help us more.

At this precious time of conversation with the Triune God and His *entourage,* we need to have faith. We have to be convinced that they look at us and love us in spite of our weaknesses and sins, provided that we are truthfully sorry for these transgressions. The Lord is always there—even when we do not "feel" His presence at all.

In other words, we should not converse with God for the sake of experiencing enjoyment and sensible consolations; but rather to please Him: the Lord is to replace our ego. If we adopt this attitude, we will persevere in prayer even if it turns out to be a dry and arid experience. St. Josemaría puts it this way: "Don't tell Jesus you want consolation in prayer. But if He gives it to you, thank Him. Tell Him always that what you want is perseverance [in prayer]."[30] Yes, oftentimes we will need to remember the complaint of our Lord in Gethsemane: "Simon, are you asleep? Could you not watch one hour?"[31]

As a good-humored friend of mine once told me, "It is obvious that the purpose of going to pray is not just to feel good, for if this were the case, I

---

30 Ibid., no. 100.
31 Mk 14:37.

would expect spiritual writers to recommend going to prayer with a bottle of liquor, not just with a spiritual book." And as to make his point clearer, he added in the same vein:

> There is the story of a businessman who, at noon, went to the Manila cathedral to spend some time in meditation. It was hot, and since it was after lunch, he felt quite sleepy and told our Lord that he was leaving for he was feeling very far and disconnected from Him. As he was walking towards the door of the church, the organist had started his daily rehearsal, and upon hearing the notes of that beautiful music, he decided to stay, and he told our Lord, "Now I feel very near You!"
>
> Unfortunately, however, after a few minutes there was a brown-out, and the electric organ fell silent. And so did the businessman's feelings who, turning towards the sanctuary, said, "Lord, I feel far from You again! I am leaving!"

My friend commented that he deserved to have heard a voice coming from the tabernacle telling him, "Come on, do not be so superficial, don't subordinate your prayer life to Meralco!"[32]

The point here is that even though such things as music could help elicit feelings that facilitate prayer, they are not to be taken as an essential and indispensable element for our conversation with Him. What is essential is *faith* that leads to love

---

[32] An electric company that supplies electricity to the residents of the city of Manila.

and hope. With or without feelings, we can always love. For this reason, in prayer, love matters more than thinking. Love benefits from feelings as well as from dryness, from inspirations as well as from aridity. Anything that fosters our love for God is a good subject matter for our prayer.

We see examples of this in the life of our Lord as recorded in the Gospels. We can talk with Him about what is happening to us in our lives in a very natural way, and silently seek His advice for the decisions we are going to make. What matters most is some awareness—savory fruit of faith—that we are in the presence of the Lord of Lords, as well as of His supernatural *entourage*. Consequently, words are not always needed. We could, at times, simply *give silent company* to the personages of the supernatural world.

On several occasions, the founder of Opus Dei emphasized that there are countless ways of praying. But he would like everyone to pray genuinely, as God's children, not gabbling away like hypocrites who will hear from Jesus' lips: "Not everyone who says to me, 'Lord, Lord!' shall enter into the kingdom of heaven."[33] When we cry "Lord!" we must do so with a desire to put into practice the inspirations the Holy Spirit awakens in our soul.

What is truly important in prayer is to place oneself in His presence and to try to remain there. To this effect, it would help to slowly repeat the introductory prayer mentioned above, time and again, until its message registers in our soul. The idea is to become fully aware that right now, the veiled God is

---

[33] Mt 7:21.

here, in front of me, or at my side, or inside of me, for in fact He is everywhere. "It is always possible to enter into inner prayer, independently of the conditions of health, work or emotional state. The heart is the place of this quest and encounter, in poverty and in faith."[34]

Naturally, our spiritual contact with our Lord will enkindle in us a great desire to improve our lives in return for His overwhelming Love. In other words, it will move us to make some specific resolutions to behave much better in the future. In addition, it will move us to perform good deeds, especially those that benefit others, as a practical manifestation of our love for God.

The greatest fruit of this contact with the Lord is that our heart has grown in love for Him, and our commitment to Christ will have become deeper. He said: "I came to cast fire upon earth; and would that it were already kindled!"[35] In prayer, in this conversation with God, we find the strength to overcome tiredness and to reject tepidity.

Moreover, intimacy with God will result in a greater determination to resist temptations and a more persevering apostolic zeal; that is, a bigger eagerness to happily share with others the fruits of our prayer and contemplation. All along, we are convinced that all the sincere prayers are heard, that they are never useless, although they are not always granted in the way we would like.

Consequently, as suggested by St. Josemaría, we could end the period of conversation with Jesus by telling Him:

---

[34] *Catechism of the Catholic Church*, no. 2710.
[35] Lk 12:49.

I give you thanks, my God, for the good resolutions, affections and inspirations you have communicated to me in this meditation. I beg your help in performing them. My Immaculate Mother, St. Joseph my father and lord, my guardian angel, intercede for me.

This invocation to our Immaculate Mother responds to the great need we have for her help. She is the mother of all Christians—among other reasons—because when she carried our Savior in her womb, she was also carrying all those whose lives were united to Jesus Christ's life.

The *Catechism of the Catholic Church*, a great gift of God to His Spouse and Mystical Body, has devoted a good number of very helpful pages to the subject of prayer. Here are some excerpts taken from them:

- **Prayer** is the raising of one's mind and heart to God or the requesting of good things to God. But when we pray, do we speak from the heights of our pride and will, or "out of the depths" of a humble and contrite heart? Only when we humbly acknowledge that "we do not know how to pray as we ought" are we ready to receive freely the gift of prayer. "Man is a beggar before God" (St. Augustine) (no. 2590).[36]

- God tirelessly calls each person to this mysterious encounter with Himself. Prayer unfolds

---

[36] "Christian prayer is a covenant relationship between God and man in Christ. It is the action of God and of man, springing from both the Holy Spirit and ourselves, wholly directed to the Father, in union with the human will of the Son of God made man" (no. 2564).

throughout the whole history of salvation as a reciprocal call between God and man (no. 2594).[37]

- Jesus' filial prayer is the perfect model of prayer in the New Testament. Often done in solitude and in secret, the prayer of Jesus involves adherence to the will of the Father even to the Cross and an absolute confidence in being heard.[38]

- Our Lord gave us an example on how to find time and a proper place for prayer in the midst of a busy schedule, and surrounded by crowds eager to be with Him. "And rising up long before daybreak, He went out and departed into a desert place, and there He prayed."[39] Moreover, He often escaped to the mountainside to be able to communicate with His heavenly Father. We might have to do similar things in our modern and hectic setting.

- The prayers of the Virgin Mary, in her *Fiat* and *Magnificat*, are characterized by the generous offering of her whole being in faith (no. 2622).

....

[37] "In the New Covenant, prayer is the living relationship of the children of God with their Father who is good beyond measure, with His Son, Jesus Christ and with the Holy Spirit. (...) This communion of life is always possible because, through Baptism, we have already been united with Christ" (no. 2565).

[38] "In His teaching, Jesus teaches His disciples to pray with a purified heart, with lively and persevering faith, with filial boldness. He calls them to vigilance and invites them to present their petitions to God in His name. Jesus Christ Himself answers prayers addressed to Him" (no. 2621).

[39] Mk 1:35.

[Mary is a model of trustful prayer, as evidenced at the wedding in Cana.][40]

When we offer prayers of petition, Leo Trese explains:

> Asking God for our needs, we are not of course telling God something that He does not know. God knows what we need far better than we know ourselves; He has known all our needs from all eternity. A prayer of petition for ourselves focuses our attention on our own necessity and keeps alive our awareness of God's goodness; in prayers of petition for others, we are given the opportunity for limitless acts of charity.[41]

St. Thomas Aquinas further clarifies that prayer of petition makes us stop and realize our own smallness, and desire the thing we are praying for in a fervent, filial spirit. Thus, we become more worthy to receive it.

---

[40] "**Adoration** is the first attitude of man acknowledging that he is a creature before his Creator. It exalts the greatness of the Lord who made us and the almighty power of the Savior who sets us free from evil. Adoration is homage of the spirit to the 'King of Glory'; respectful silence in the presence of the 'ever greater' God" (no. 2628).
"**Praise** is the form of prayer which recognizes most immediately that God is God. It lauds God for His own sake and gives Him glory, quite beyond what He does, but simply because He is (…). Praise embraces the other forms of prayer and carries them toward Him who is its source and goal: the one God, the Father, from whom are all things and for whom we exist" (no. 2639).

[41] Leo Trese, *The Faith Explained* (Manila: Sinag-tala Publishers, 2008), 537.

Our Lord Himself directed us to pray perseveringly, "We ought always to pray and not to lose heart."[42] And He also pointed out the importance to pray together with others, "If two of you agree on earth about anything they ask, it will be done for them by my Father in heaven."[43]

Our prayer of petition should be persevering and patient. We should not get discouraged because we do not get what we ask for right away. The veiled God nearly always wishes to uphold His condition of a sheltered Lord; wants to give us the chance to earn merits upon testing our faith; and allows us to manifest our trust and perseverance. It took St. Monica fourteen years of fervent prayer to obtain the conversion of her son Augustine.

Moreover, it should also be full of trust. Pope Benedict XVI has said: "Every prayer, no matter its imperfections, reaches God. There are no superfluous, useless, prayers, not one of them is lost."[44, 45]

....

[42] Lk 18:1.

[43] Mt 18:19.

[44] Benedict XVI, General Audience, Sep. 12, 2012.

[45] "**Thanksgiving** characterizes the prayer of the Church which, in celebrating the Eucharist, reveals and becomes more fully what she is. The thanksgiving of the Body participates in that of their Head [Jesus Christ]. The letters of St. Paul often begin and end with thanksgiving: 'Give thanks in all circumstances; for this is the will of God in Christ Jesus for you'" (no. 2637, 2638).
Atonement is another kind of prayer. By it, we acknowledge our sinfulness; we beg God's pardon for our infidelity and make amendments for the debt of punishment that we have incurred. It is also called prayer of reparation. "Nothing is so efficacious in appeasing God, when His wrath is kindled; nothing so effectively delays or averts

Expressions of Prayer

Vocal **prayer** is an essential element of the Christian life. To His disciples, drawn by their master's silent prayer, Jesus teaches a vocal prayer, the *Our Father*. He not only prayed aloud the liturgical prayers of the synagogue but, as the gospels show, He raised his voice to express His personal prayer, from exultant blessing of the father to the agony of Gethsemane (CCC no. 2701).

The need to involve the sense in interior prayer corresponds to a requirement of our human nature. We are body and spirit, and we experience the need to translate our feelings externally. We must pray with our

---

the punishments prepared for the wicked as the prayers of men" (St. Jerome).

"By **prayer of petition** we express awareness of our relationship with God. We are creatures who are not our own beginning, not the masters of adversary, not our own last end. We are sinners who as Christians know we have turned away from our Father. Our petition is already a turning back to Him" (no. 2629).

"**Intercession** is a prayer of petition which leads us to pray as Jesus did. He is the intercessor with the Father on behalf of all men, especially sinners. The Holy Spirit himself intercedes for us" (no. 2634).

"**The Holy Mass**, the Eucharist, contains and expresses all forms of prayer: it is 'the pure offering' of the whole Body of Christ to the glory of God's name and, according to the tradition of East and West, it is the 'sacrifice of praise'" (no. 2643).

whole being, to give all power possible to our supplication (no. 2702).

Meditation is above all a quest [engaging thought, imagination, emotion and desire]. The mind seeks to understand the why and how of the Christian life, in order to adhere and stand to what the Lord is asking. The required attentiveness is difficult to sustain. We are usually helped by books (no. 2705).

To meditate on what we read helps us to make it our own by confronting it ourselves. Here, another book is opened: the book of life. We pass from thought to reality. To the extent that we are humble and faithful, we discover in meditation the movements that stir the heart and we are able to discern them. It is a question of acting truthfully in order to come up into the light, "Lord, what is it that You want of me?" (no. 2706).

What is *contemplative prayer?* St. Teresa answers, "Contemplative prayer, in my opinion, is nothing else than a close sharing between friends; it means taking time frequently to be alone with Him who we know loves us."

Contemplative prayer seeks Him "Whom my soul loves." It is Jesus, and in Him, the Father, we seek Him because to desire Him is always the beginning of love, and we seek Him in that pure faith which causes us to be born of Him and to live in Him (no. 2709).

Entering into contemplative prayer is like entering into the Eucharistic liturgy [Holy Mass]: we "gather up" the heart, recollect our whole being under the prompting of the Holy Spirit, abide in the dwelling place of the Lord which we are, awaken our faith in order to enter into the presence of Him who awaits us. We let our masks fall and turn our hearts back to the Lord who loves us, so as to hand ourselves over to Him as an offering to be purified and transformed (no. 2711).

Contemplative prayer is the prayer of the child of God, of the forgiven sinner who agrees to welcome the love by which he is loved and who wants to respond to it by loving even more. But he knows that the love he is returning is poured out by the Spirit in his heart, for everything is grace [gift] from God. Contemplative prayer is the poor and humble surrender to the loving will of the Father in ever deeper union with His beloved Son (no. 2712).

Contemplation is a *gaze* of faith, fixed on Jesus. "I look at Him and He looks at me": this is what a certain peasant of Ars used to say to his holy curé about his prayer before the tabernacle. This focus on Jesus is a renunciation of self. His gaze purifies our heart; the light of the countenance of Jesus illumines the eyes of our heart and teaches us to see everything in the light of His truth and His compassion for all men (no. 2715).

Contemplative prayer is *hearing* the Word of God. Far from being passive, such attentiveness is the obedience of faith, the unconditional acceptance of a servant and the loving commitment of a child. It participates in the "Yes" of the Son become servant and the *Fiat* of God's lowly handmaid (no. 2716).

Contemplative prayer is a *union* with the prayer of Christ insofar as it makes us participate in His mystery (no. 2718).

Contemplative prayer is a communion of love bearing Life for the multitude, to the extent that it consents to abide in the night of faith (no. 2719).

The Battle of Prayer

Prayer is both a gift and a determined response on our part. It always presupposes effort. Prayer is a battle against ourselves and against the wiles of the tempter who does all he can to turn man away from prayer, away from union with God (no. 2725).

In the battle of prayer, we must face *erroneous notions of prayer*. Some people view prayer as a simple psychological activity, others as an effort of concentration to reach a mental void. Still others reduce prayer to ritual words and postures. Many Christians unconsciously regard prayer as an occupation that is incompatible with all the other things they have to do: they "don't have the time" (no. 2726).

Finally, our battle has to confront what we experience as *failure in prayer:* discouragement during periods of dryness; sadness that, because we have "great possessions," we have not given them all to the Lord; disappointment over not being heard according to our own will; wounded pride, stiffened by the indignity that is ours as sinners; our resistance to the idea that prayer is a free and unmerited gift; and so forth. The conclusion is always the same: what good does it do to pray? To overcome these obstacles, we must battle to gain humility, trust, and perseverance (no. 2728).

Facing Difficulties in Prayer

The principal difficulties in the practice of prayer are distraction and dryness. The remedy lies *in faith, conversion, and vigilance of heart* (no. 2754).

Two frequent difficulties threaten prayer: *lack of faith and laziness for spiritual things (acedia)*—a form of depression stemming from lax ascetical practices that lead to discouragement (no. 2755).

Filial trust is put to the test when we feel that our prayer is not always heard. The Gospel invites us to ask ourselves about the conformity of our prayer to the desire of the Spirit (no. 2756).

Pray constantly (1 Thess 5:17), always and for everything giving thanks in the name of our Lord Jesus Christ to God the Father. It is always possible to pray. It is even a vital necessity. Prayer and Christian life are inseparable (no. 2757).

St. Paul adds, "Pray at all times in the Spirit, with all prayer and supplication. To that end keep alert with all perseverance making supplication for all the saints" (no. 2742).

The Perfect Sacrificial Meal

After this, the Holy Mass begins. We are aware that it is the greatest action we will take part on that day, as well as the best gift that we, in union with Jesus and with the help of the Holy Spirit, can offer to the veiled God the Father. Therefore, in order to be there and to participate in the Holy Sacrifice, we do not hesitate to exert a considerable effort. We realize that it is something truly worthwhile. At the offertory, when the priest lifts up the paten, you imagine that you place on it all your efforts for the day.

Truly, the Holy Mass is the bloodless re-presentation of the Sacrifice at Calvary. In the Eucharistic Sacrifice and on the Cross, there is the same Eternal Priest and the same Victim of Calvary, Jesus Christ, truly present! Regardless of who is officiating on the altar, the High Priest of every Mass is our Lord Himself. Only He has the divine power to change ordinary bread into His Body, and plain wine into His precious Blood. He transcends time and space.

As an effective and sensible sign, the Holy Mass is also the sacramental memorial of the Last Supper and of the Resurrection of Jesus. In Holy Communion, we receive not only the Body of Christ, but also the Risen Lord. It is, therefore, the sacramental memorial of the Paschal Mystery: Passion, Death, and Resurrection of Christ. By it, the sacrifice of the Cross is perpetuated over the centuries. It is, therefore, at the same time and inseparably, the sacrificial commemoration of the sacrifice of the Cross, and the sacred banquet by which we have a most intimate communion with the Lord's Body and Blood.

Antonio María Ramírez, a noted Spanish priest, puts it this way:

> We Christians have an unconquerable force: Christ has defeated sin and has changed the meaning of death and we are reminded of this splendid reality in the Holy Mass. On the altar of the world, in any place, at any time, Jesus climbs up to the Cross. There is nothing better.[46]

The Holy Mass is the perfect sacrifice of adoration, thanksgiving, petition, and reparation offered by Jesus Christ to His eternal Father by the action of the Holy Spirit, and the instrumental cooperation of the priest celebrating, in which Jesus acts in His capacity as the Eternal High Priest and Head of His Mystical Body, the Church.

In view of this, it is not surprising that the first of the Church's Commandments is: "On Sundays and

---

[46] Antonio María Ramírez, *Comprometerse*, 58.

other holy days of obligation, the faithful are bound to participate in the Mass."[47] The Church commands this observance as a minimum and under pain of mortal sin, an indication of how important the Holy Mass is for our spiritual life and our inner growth.

Although mankind all over the world persists in offending God very grievously, the continuous offering of Holy Masses offers a mighty ray of hope, for in every Holy Mass Jesus tells His heavenly Father: "Forgive them; for they know not what they do."[48] This realization moved St. Leonard to state:

> I believe that were it not for Holy Mass, at this moment the world would be in the abyss, unable to bear the mighty load of its iniquities. The Holy Mass is the potent prop that holds the world upon its base.

> Therefore, when we are participating in it, we ought to do that which once the Portuguese Admiral Alphonse of Albuquerque did, who, finding himself with his fleet in danger of perishing during a fierce and terrific tempest, adopted the following means: He took in his arms an innocent child which was on board his ship, and lifting him up towards heaven, he said, "If we are sinners, this creature is certainly free from sin; Lord, for love of this innocent, remit to us the death we deserve!" Will you believe it? The spectacle of that stainless babe was so pleasing to the Lord that He tranquilized the sea, and changed into joy for these unfortunates

---

[47] *Catechism of the Catholic Church*, no. 2180.
[48] Lk 23:34.

their terror of a death already imminent. Now what do you believe is done by the Eternal Father when the priest, lifting in the air the thrice sacred Victim, shows to Him the innocence of His divine Son? Then His compassion cannot resist the sight of the most spotless innocence of Jesus, and He feels as if compelled to calm our storms, and to provide for all our necessities.[49]

In the words of Pope St. John Paul II: "The Eucharistic Sacrifice is the source and summit of all Christian Life. It is a single sacrifice that embraces everything. It is the greatest treasure of the Church. It is Her life."[50]

Accordingly, St. Josemaría Escrivá says, "It brings us face to face with one of the central mysteries of our faith, because it is the gift of the Blessed Trinity to the Church. It is because of this that we can consider the Mass as the center and the source of a Christian's spiritual life."[51]

St. Josemaría advises:

Think about the Holy Mass—how we should celebrate or attend it. Consider how the Angels are there. Consider that what you are doing or taking part in is something divine. Think how, on the altar, Christ is offering Himself once more for you and for me. And

---

[49] St. Leonard of Port Maurice, *The Hidden Treasure of the Holy Mass* (Rockford, Illinois: TAN Books and Publishers, Inc., 1952) (back cover).

[50] John Paul II, *Prayer for Priests on Holy Thursday*, March 25, 1982, https://w2.vatican.va/content/john-paul-ii/en/letters/1982.index.2.html.

[51] *Christ is Passing By*, no. 87.

you will earnestly desire to imitate Him in His humility, in the way He empties Himself completely in the Host; and you will be filled with thanksgiving and adoration, desires of reparation, and petitions. You will offer yourself up, your arms outstretched, as another Christ, *ipse Christus* (Christ Himself), ready to be nailed to the sweet wood of the Cross for love of souls.[52]

At the beginning of the Holy Mass, there were on the altar simple bread and plain wine. After the consecration, the Risen Christ is present, alive, with His sacred Body, His spotless Soul, and His infinite divinity. What a sublime change! Should we not be most eager to be there when it happens? It is worthwhile to make some sacrifice; it will never be comparable with His sacrifice on Calvary.

This change is effected by the Holy Spirit for our sake. Our Lord wants to be our nourishment. When we receive Holy Communion, it is not the Eucharist that is transformed into us, but we are the ones who become spiritually united to Christ. St. Augustine attributes these words to our Lord: "You will not convert Me into yourself, as you transform food into your own flesh: you will be changed into Me."[53]

In light of these considerations, it stands to reason that we would want to be with our Lord by:

- Always coming to Holy Mass on time. It is a very good idea to make the Sunday Holy Mass a family

---

[52] St. Josemaría Escrivá, *Notes taken from a meditation*, April 14, 1960.

[53] St. Augustine, *Confessions* (New York: Image Books, 1960), no. 7, 10.

event. This should not be the reason, however, for any lack of punctuality. It is a way of being considerate with Jesus Christ and with others who are attending the Eucharistic Sacrifice.

- Dressing properly and modestly. It is a matter of realizing that we are meeting with the King of Kings. Women, especially, are to refrain from dressing in such a way that they could lead others to sin. They are to recall that our Lord said: "Everyone who looks at a woman lustfully has already committed adultery with her in his heart."[54]

- Genuflecting and bowing reverently at the proper places and at the proper time and by standing, sitting, and kneeling *with* the congregation.

- Maintaining reverent silence and a dignified posture inside the church. We should avoid, for example, receiving Holy Communion in the mouth while having the hands in the pockets— it is too casual and not a respectful attitude. We would not approach and face a high dignitary in this way.

Above all, we are to make sure that our Holy Communion will be a worthy one. Bear in mind these words of St. Paul:

> Therefore whoever eats this bread or drinks the cup of the Lord unworthily, will be guilty of the body and the blood of our Lord. But let a man prove himself, and so let him eat of the bread and drink of the cup; for he who eats and drinks unworthily, without

---

[54] Mt 5:28.

distinguishing the body, eats and drinks judgment to himself.[55]

We are to also bear in mind that although it is very good to receive Holy Communion during the Holy Mass, it is only required for the priest celebrating. The faithful in the congregation are not required to do so by the laws of the Church. Even without partaking of the Holy Communion, participating in the Holy Mass has a great value, significance, and beneficial effects.

- Participating actively by uniting ourselves to the Holy Sacrifice at the altar, we are to follow the rites of the Holy Mass, and receive Holy Communion while observing the Eucharistic fast, with a conscience that does not accuse us of any mortal sin. Writes Ronald Knox: "The Holy Eucharist is a sun which fosters supernatural life in those who receive it worthily, rain which gives them growth. It is a sun which dries up all life in the souls which receive it unworthily, rain which brings it only corruption."[56]

We are to correspond to the love of Christ who expressed thus His desire to institute the Eucharist: *"I have greatly desired to eat this Passover with you before I suffer."*[57] We rightfully express our gratitude to anyone who pays the tiniest service to us. Should we not show much more appreciation to our Lord for the Bread of Life?

---

[55] 1 Cor 11: 29.
[56] Ronald Knox, *A Retreat for Lay People* (Lagos: Criterion Publications, 2005), 85.
[57] Lk 22:15.

- Putting electronic phones and other devices in silent mode. To answer a phone call or sending text messages during Holy Mass are irreverent acts.

- Maintaining respectful silence inside the church at all times.

- Staying in the church until the Holy Mass is concluded, and preferably after giving thanks, for about ten minutes. "It should be pointed out to the faithful that, after the Eucharistic banquet, they ought not to neglect to make a sincere and fitting thanksgiving."[58]

If we do so, the Eucharistic Sacrifice will have an effect in our ordinary life. We, for instance, will work with greater motivation, we will treat others more charitably, and we will have the joy proper of a son or a daughter of God.

Work as Usual

Now, the time has come to go to work. This means facing the traffic situation again. It is rush hour and everyone seems to be tense. But the period of prayer has helped you a lot for this new challenge. Maybe a taxicab or a motorcycle has come from nowhere, gotten in your way, and suddenly forced you to apply the brakes. You were tempted to curse the bones of the driver, but you then remembered that besides bones, he has a soul to save. So,

----

[58] Sacred Congregation of Divine Worship, *Immensae Caritatis*, Jan. 29, 1973, no.3.

you say a prayer for him: "Lord, help that driver to do a better job, he needs it badly!" And aware that getting mad would not solve any problem, you repress other less supernatural ideas and words that might spontaneously occur to you.

You have arrived at your place of work. There you find the same setting as every day: the same faces, the same furniture around, the same environment day in and day out. It might appear prosaic and unappealing, and yet, it is precisely *there,* and not somewhere else, that the great Spectator wants you to perform for Him and for the entire supernatural Audience. It can become an exciting experience if there is enough faith, hope, and love.

Perhaps you find your colleagues at work chatting before beginning their daily tasks. You, in contrast, are eager to begin to sanctify that work by beginning on time and doing it well, with all the human perfection that you are capable of. For you, punctuality is an important element of good working habits. You have a motivation others seem to lack: you are conscious of the fact that you are being constantly looked at by your loving Father. Others are, perhaps, talking negatively about some absent people. You profoundly dislike backbiting, not only because it is unfair, since those persons cannot defend themselves, but because it offends the veiled Father who loves everyone and wants us to do the same. Upon seizing the situation, convinced that just because something is very "common" does not mean that it is "right," you try to find a way to improve the topic of the conversation.

The long daily hours of work have begun. It is a good moment to renew the gift of that labor you made in the morning offering and in the Holy Mass when you mentally placed on the paten—lifted up by the priest—the work you would carry out during the day. That offering covers all your labor: those things you enjoy doing, as well as the tedious tasks done hour after hour, and also the frustrations and periods of pressure and stress. It also covers the unforeseen happenings that challenge your cool and try your patience. Once more, the teachings of the founder of Opus Dei are of help:

> You are upset. Look: happen what may in your interior life or in the world around you, never forget that the importance of events or of people is very relative. Take things calmly. Let time pass. And then, as you view persons and events dispassionately and from afar, you'll acquire the perspective that will enable you to see each thing in its proper place and in its true proportion. If you do this, you will be more objective and you'll be spared yourself many causes of anxiety.[59]

Through work, you joyfully cooperate with God to make this world a better place to live in and you contribute positively in Jesus' work of Redemption. You do not want to forget that line in the book of Job: "Man is born to labor and the bird to fly."[60] For you, work is an obligation rooted in human nature. It was planned by God from the very beginning, even before the fall from Paradise. The Lord placed man in the world "so that he would work."[61] It is clear

---

[59] *The Way*, no. 702.
[60] Job 5:7.
[61] Gen 3:19 (*Ut operaretur*).

that work is a good thing for man, because through work man not only transforms nature, adapting it to his needs, but also achieves fulfillment as a human being.

St. Benedict, an ancient saint, has left us an excellent motto as a guide in our journey: Pray and Work! (*Ora et Labora!*) finds an echo in the teachings of St. Josemaría, a saint of the twentieth century.

It is obvious that some people work much and very well, but they do not pray. It is a pity, for they seem to have forgotten that none can please God without praying, as expressed in the words of the Master, "What does it profit a man if he gains the whole world, but ruin or lose himself?" (Lk 9:25).

There are also people who pray much, but do not work. God does not approve of this either. They are sometimes called "Holy Joes" or "do-gooders," and they do not command respect. Finally, there are others who neither work nor pray. They are, surely, the least pleasing to God.

A true Christian adopts and practices the Benedictine motto, combining the two virtues of prayer and work in unity of life.

Jesus, Mary, and Joseph have left us with a very impressive example of dedication to work. Thus, if out of laziness someone refuses to labor, he or she cannot properly call himself or herself Christian. St. Paul's dictum is well known: "If someone does not want to work, he should not eat." St. Josemaría writes, "You must strive for holiness, contributing at the same time to the sanctification of others, your fellow men; sanctifying your work and your environment."[62] In a summarized form, these ideas could be expressed saying that *we are to sanctify our ordinary work, sanctify ourselves in our work, and sanctify others with our work.*

The founder of Opus Dei says, "If we really want to sanctify our work, we are inescapably to fulfill the first condition: that of working well, with human and supernatural seriousness."[63]

In order to sanctify ourselves in our profession or trade, we ought to work seeking the glory of God. This implies a steady exercise of supernatural and human virtues. This seemingly monotonous, and perhaps small task, has a transcendent value of co-redemption and is very valuable in God's eyes; that is *faith*. Similarly, *hope* that we will be able to achieve union with God, precisely in and through these daily tasks. And, as the crowning virtue, *charity*, that inclines us to do everything for the love of God.

After that, follow a host of moral virtues: *Prudence*, that facilitates determining the proper means to apply at every instance in order to obtain the right objective; *Justice*, that leads us to give to each one his or her due and to fulfill our familial, professional, and social duties; *Temperance*, a virtue that helps us moderate our tendency to enjoy pleasurable things in excess; *Fortitude*, that allows us to persevere in fulfilling our professional duties, even when they become strenuous and difficult; *Humility*, which facilitates seeking, in all our endeavors, not our personal satisfaction, but God's glory. We could mention many other virtues such as *order, punctuality*, and *industriousness*.

---

[62] *Christ Is Passing By*, no. 46.
[63] *The Forge*, no. 698.

Thus, motivated by love, above all by divine love, we are moved to work and spend ourselves for others.

Working much and well is also a means to apostolize, to bring others closer to God. It is a universally recognized fact that people value a job done well. Our Lord impressed His contemporaries who exclaimed: "He did everything well!"[64]

Work has great importance. As a task of collaboration and stewardship with the Creator, it is a way to make this world a more humane and livable place, to contribute to a more just social order, and to pursue the temporal common good. In addition, work is also a means and an opportunity to apostolize. It is a *hook* to *fish* souls for Christ. When a colleague at work struggles to be united to God, to take Christ seriously, he often moves others like him to do the same.

A Date at Noon

Noon time is a welcome break. It is a golden opportunity to be faithful to a very brief and punctual *date* with our Blessed Mother.

The *Angelus*[65] is a wonderful and ancient practice introduced in 1263. It has a long history behind it. In our times, the pope appears at noon on Sundays

---

[64] Mk 7:37.
[65] According to ancient usage, the *Angelus* can be said at 6:00 am, 12:00 noon, and 6:00 pm, depending on the customs of the place. During Easter time, the *Regina Coeli* (Queen of Heaven) is said instead. This is a hymn of joy over the Resurrection of Our Lord.

at St. Peter's Square in Vatican City to pray the *Angelus* with those who have gathered there. In so doing, the Holy Father gives us an example on keeping proper priorities. He interrupts whatever he is doing in order to honor the Virgin Mary. It is an invitation to us to act in a similar fashion while involved in our daily occupations.

The *Angelus* is a way to cross the *barrier*—exercising our faith—and to converse with Our Lady on the role she played in our redemption. We remind her of the great moment of the Annunciation when the Archangel Gabriel made known to her God's plan of salvation, and her most exceptional vocation to be the Mother of God. We also remind her and ourselves of her splendid surrender, expressed by her words, "Be it done to me according to your word!"[66] which made us brothers of Jesus Christ and heirs of heaven. In short, we bring to our mind the sublime mystery of the Incarnation.

From Easter Sunday to Pentecost Sunday, the "Queen of Heaven" (*Regina Coeli*) is said instead of the *Angelus*.

We can check at this point, after the short noon stop, how we are faring in the fulfillment of the resolutions concerning the examination of some aspects of our spiritual life.

---

[66] Cf. Lk 1:26-38.

Bringing Friends Closer to God

Lunch time is often an excellent opportunity to eat with colleagues and friends, interact, and deepen our bond with them. Before eating, we say a short prayer to ask God to bless us and the food that we are about to eat. Afterwards, it is fitting to say a prayer to express to Him our gratitude for all the benefits we are receiving.

Lunch is a good occasion to interact with friends, to know their concerns, and to give useful advice in professional as well as spiritual matters. With the help of the Guardian Angel, you can do an effective apostolate of friendship and trust. The founder of Opus Dei says, "Win over the guardian angel of the one you want to draw to your apostolate. He is always a great accomplice."[67]

At the workplace where much of your time is spent, you meet different kinds of people. Some are a joy to deal with, others not so much. You manage to meet all of them with a smile. Perhaps, on occasion, someone misunderstands or maltreats you, and you then recall these words of St. Josemaría, "All right: that person has behaved badly toward you. But, haven't you behaved worse toward God?"[68]

In this manner, you manage to carry out the tasks of everyday life with order and serenity and without nervousness. You avoid haste in your gestures, even in the way you climb the stairs. You

---

[67] *The Way*, no. 563.
[68] Ibid., no. 686.

move the way you would expect from a person with a contemplative spirit. Consequently, those working with you enjoy your company, and perceive you as someone who exudes peace and happiness. If they were to seek the source of it, they would find it in your union and frequent dealings with the veiled Lord who dwells in secret but continues telling everyone: "Peace be with you!"

After a long day of toil, working intensely and orderly, it is not surprising to feel fatigued. We may be tempted to call it a day and abandon the task a bit before its time. A crucifix, or some other discreet human device on the table or place of work comes in very handy:

> You ask me, "Why that wooden Cross?" And I quote from a letter, "As I raise my eyes from the microscope, my sight comes to rest on the Cross—black and empty. That Cross without a Corpus is a symbol; it has a meaning others won't see. And I, tired out and on the point of abandoning my work, once again bring my eyes close to the lens and continue. For that lonely Cross is calling for a pair of shoulders to bear it."[69]

With your good behavior, without any fuss, with all naturalness, you are setting an example. After some time, the situation in the workplace has improved. Thus, the call of St. Josemaría has been fulfilled: "To sanctify work, to sanctify yourself in work, and to sanctify others through work."[70]

----

[69] Ibid., no. 277.
[70] Josemaría Escrivá, *Conversations with Msgr. Escrivá de Balaguer* (Manila: Sinag-tala Publishers, 1972), 14.

A Very Important Visit

appily, the time to go home has now come. Recalling that our Lord came to you in Holy Communion during the Holy Mass in the morning, you deem it appropriate to return that visit by going to the Blessed Sacrament at some other moment of the day, perhaps, on your way back home. It is a way of giving thanks to the veiled Lover. Maybe there is a church or adoration chapel on your way. A little research on this matter will facilitate things. Perhaps there could be a chapel of a Catholic school or hospital where the Eucharistic Lord is waiting for you in the tabernacle. He is there fulfilling what He promised on the day of His Ascension to heaven: "Behold I am with you all days, even unto the consummation of the world."[71]

He is always there: patient, silent, and waiting for some attention. St. Josemaría tells us, "When you approach the tabernacle, remember that He has been waiting for you for twenty centuries."[72] Upon instituting the Eucharist, He has wanted to share His life with ours.

He is a veiled Lover; the veil on the tabernacle is a reminder of this fact. He is there giving us a striking and permanent proof of His immense Love that calls for reciprocation. This visit does not require much time. In addition to your spontaneous prayers, you might choose to say three times each the Our

---

[71] Mt 28:20
[72] The Way, no. 537.

Father, Hail Mary, and Glory Be. At the end, make a Spiritual Communion such as this one, which St. Josemaría liked and recommended: "I wish, Lord, to receive You with the purity, humility, and devotion with which Your most holy Mother received You, with the spirit and fervor of the saints."

It is a sterling prayer that can be said anytime, anywhere. There are also occasions in which we are particularly prompted to say a Spiritual Communion, such as, for instance, when we pass in front of a Catholic church, a school or hospital, or any place where we know our Lord is in a tabernacle. There are many opportunities to give the veiled Lover some consolation.

As St. Josemaría observes, "The frequency of our visits to the Lord is in proportion to two factors: faith and the involvement of the heart; seeing the truth and loving it."[73] Jesus has remained in the Sacred Host for us so as to stay by our side, to sustain us, to guide us. And love can only be repaid with love.

How could we not turn to the Blessed Sacrament each day, even if it is only for a few minutes, "to bring Him our greetings and our love as children and as brothers?"[74]

In many cases, even if we have a busy daily schedule, a visit to the *"Prisoner of Love"* can be made, and it will do wonders to our spiritual life. The reason is clear: we behave much better when we are conscious of the presence, the glance, the company, and the love of Christ.

---

[73] *Furrow*, no. 818.

[74] Ibid., no. 686.

Sanctifying Home Life

A rriving home is a delight. Those you love so much and for whom you have been toiling all day long are waiting for your arrival. Many times throughout the day you have been entrusting them to the silent Lord and to others in His entourage: "Lord, for Pete who is taking an exam today, or for Agnes who is applying for a job this afternoon." Now they are all here and you are going to give yourself to them, even though you are very tired. You will still volunteer to go out to buy medicine for the one who is coughing, or to repair an appliance that is not functioning well. You realize, of course, that there is no reason why you should feel and act like a hero for doing these small things. But you know that if you do them with, and for, the love of the veiled Witness of your life, they become incredibly valuable, for they acquire the merit of Love. And if you persevere in doing them this way, they will end up sanctifying you.

Perhaps, you are reading the newspaper and the youngest kid approaches you and asks you a barrage of questions; or perhaps he wants to tell you everything that happened at school. If you were to set the newspaper aside and attend to these trifles, it might be written in your book of life as something very positive and the great Proctor will be very pleased.

You have built an atmosphere of trust at home. You see to it that your kids are not so afraid of you to think that they need to have recourse to lying when they did something wrong. They could own the lyrics of the old song, "Oh My Papa," and say about you: "He always understood." They may find you demanding, yes, but consistently reasonable and considerate. Above all, they perceive you as approachable. You are not overly afraid of losing your authority over your children. They can speak to you as a friend about everything, even intimate and personal matters, such as a "crush" they are experiencing.

You love sharing activities with the members of your family. You enjoy doing, together with your kids, some of the hobbies they like. You know how to laugh with them, and you are interested in their studies and other concerns.

In our time, in which everyone seems to be permanently immersed in his or her electronic gadget—computer, cellphone, or tablet—you make it a point to organize excursions, walks, and get-togethers in order to foster true family life. Such activities are opportunities to impart formative values in an enjoyable and natural way, not so much because of what you say but by what they see you do. For instance, they see you saying a short prayer upon starting the trip, saying grace before and after meals and, maybe, the Holy Rosary when the length of the trip calls for it. Furthermore, they see you driving well—not losing your composure when there is a tight spot, always cheerful, optimistic, and with good humor.

Javier Abad and Eugenio Fenoy put it well:

> Family get-togethers offer many opportunities for everyone to better know, understand and love each other. It is a time to talk

about small victories, of one's dreams, of taking interest in the others and becoming aware of each one's personality; it is a time to know how to adjust to each one's quirks. If parents know how to observe their children in these moments, they will be able to draw many accurate and effective educational approaches.

The get-together cannot be the time to read the newspaper, watch television or to clean the kitchen. Neither is it the time to scold someone, or to ask him to make a public account of his studies. It is the time to show affection and to crack a joke. It is the time to laugh together.[75]

One thing you might be inclined to do, but which is better not to do, is to compare one child with another sibling or classmate. The reason is simple— God has made a very unequal distribution of gifts and each one is called to play, in the great test and game of life, with the talents he or she has received, that is, with the set of cards the Lord has put in his or her hands. Comparisons are often not only odious but out of order or even senseless. Accordingly, you help your children not to compete with anybody except themselves. Thus, while encouraging each one to strive hard to be better every day, you discourage rivalry and contention.

You see to it that your home is bright and cheerful, that is, clean, simple, tidy, pleasant, warm, and

[75] Abad, Javier and Eugenio Fenoy. *Children: Their Training, Formation and Education* (Manila: Sinag-tala Publishers, 1995), p. 36.

very welcoming. In this way, everyone in the family loves to be in it. You are convinced that dirtiness, lack of aesthetic sense, and bad taste are not to be taken as indicators of the virtue of poverty. However, you have made sure that nothing extravagant or ostentatious is found in your home. You have adopted the policy of taking away useless things, and you have seen to it that all appliances, instruments, and tools are always in working condition.

You have placed some nice-looking religious items around the house, such as crucifixes and pictures of Our Lady, that discreetly preside over your family life and serve as reminders to live the presence of God. Their number, however, is not excessive; you do not want your home to resemble a shop of religious objects. In so doing, you have arranged your house as a Christian home characterized by simplicity.

Furthermore, you have fostered in your family an atmosphere of work without excessive or tension-filled stress. Everybody has his or her tasks to accomplish. A sample of such a situation is well-described in the book, *The Joys and Travails of a Large Family:*

> The eldest, who is ten years old, makes two beds in the morning before going to school. The eight-year-old girl makes two beds. The seven-year-old boy goes for milk and bread. The five-year-old girl only knows enough to dress herself, but she has to have her hair combed like the other two older ones. They gulp down their breakfast because the bus never waits for the slow ones.

At noon, the two elder girls set the table, but have no time to clear it. In the afternoon, the eldest prepares snacks for all the kids. The eight-year-old sets the table for dinner because the eldest is not yet through with her studies by that time.[76]

In this manner, your family, more so if it is numerous, has become a wonderful school of human and Christian virtues such as: dedication, loyalty, generosity, industriousness, service, and order.

Our Lady's Choice

Now that the whole family has gathered, it would be an excellent time to pray the Holy Rosary together. It is a prayer that our mother in heaven likes very much. In Lourdes, where her apparitions were endorsed by many miracles, and in Fatima, where the fulfillment of several prophesies stand as guarantors, she requested that it be prayed daily. This preference of hers should always prevail over ones of our own. Moreover, pope after pope has advised us to pray it and have enriched it with many indulgences. If the Holy Rosary is prayed as a group, a plenary indulgence may be gained.

It could be useful to pause for a few seconds to contemplate each mystery and to offer each one for a different intention. Something like: this decade is for the Holy Father; the next for my husband; for uncle Bob, who is suffering from cancer; for Louie,

---

[76] J. Lopez Navarro, *The Joys and Travails of a Large Family*. Publication details not readily available.

who is taking an exam today; for Agnes, who is reviewing to pass the board; and so on.

Some people may have to rethink their opinion about praying the Holy Rosary, just like a gentleman I came to know. He was a regular guy who excelled in sports in his younger days and was seeing me for spiritual direction once a week. He was making remarkable progress in his spiritual life.

Once, I suggested to him to start praying the Holy Rosary every day, and he surprised me with these words, "No, Father. I won't do that! When I was a young man, my mother forced me badly to pray the Rosary, and I did not like it at all. So, now that she has already passed away, I won't do it."

I paused for a while, trying to recover from my shock, and told him, "I can see that you have developed a deep dislike for this prayer, when in fact it is beautiful, Gospel-based, and centered in Christ, not just in Mary."

He nonetheless replied that he found it repetitious and monotonous. I mentioned to him what St. Josemaría wrote,

> Do you want to love our Lady? Well then, get to know her. How? By praying her Rosary well.
>
> But in the Rosary. . .we always say the same things! Always the same?
>
> And don't people in love always say the same things to each other. . . ? Might it not be that you find the Rosary monotonous because, instead of pronouncing words like a man, you mumble noises while your mind is very far from God? Moreover, listen:

before each decade we are told the mystery to be *contemplated.* Have you ever *contemplated* these mysteries?[77]

Furthermore, I even advised him to offer each decade for a different intention. For instance: first mystery for the Holy Father, second for the family, third for priests, fourth for a relative who needs much help, and so on. Nevertheless, he replied that he just did not like this prayer.

It sounded as if this was going to be the end of our exchange of ideas regarding the Holy Rosary and we had reached the end of the rope. It then occurred to me—it must have been an inspiration from the Holy Spirit—to tell him that obviously he disliked it, but Our Lady happens to like it very much. He looked at me intently and asked, "How do you know this?"

After a few seconds, I told him: "Have you heard of Lourdes? There, in 1858, Our Lady told St. Bernadette Soubirous to pray the Rosary, and at the grotto of Massabieille, Our Lady was moving the beads with her fingers. Moreover, in Fatima, in 1917, Our Lady told the little shepherds, Lucia, Jacinta, and Francisco, to pray the Holy Rosary every day. She told them this in every one of the six apparitions that happened from the month of May to the month of October. "And these," I added, "are apparitions fully endorsed by the popes and other authorities of the Church." My friend said nothing. However, the next time we met, he was sporting a big smile on his

---

[77] St. Josemaría Escrivá, *Holy Rosary* (Introduction) (Manila: Sinag-tala Publishers, 2000).

face while saying, "Father, I already pray the Rosary every day. It is not so hard!"

I was very happy with this turn of events. And not surprisingly, this friend of mine eventually joined Opus Dei, and was very faithful and grateful until his holy death. He came to understand and wholeheartedly agreed and made these parting words, from the end of St. Josemaría's book, *Holy Rosary*, his own:

> My friend: I have told you just a part of my secret. It is up to you, with God's help, to discover the rest. Take courage. Be faithful.
>
> Become little. Our Lord hides from the proud and reveals the treasures of his grace to the humble.
>
> Don't worry if, when thinking on your own, daring and childish words and affections arise in your heart. This is what Jesus wants, and Mary is encouraging you. If you say the Rosary in this way, you will learn to pray well.

The Holy Rosary is, in fact, solidly based on Sacred Scripture, being made up of many words from the Sacred texts. It is a summary of the most important events in the life of our Savior and, if prayed well, a source of many graces. It is a ladder, said Pope Paul VI, which you climb together with others stair by stair, ever getting closer to the encounter with Christ. It is a practice that brings us to Christ through the Virgin Mary. It resembles the choirs of angels in heaven who never tires of saying the self-same, "Holy, Holy, Holy," and the words of our Lord in Gethsemane, Who, "being in agony, prayed longer saying the self-same words."

The renowned American writer, Msgr. Leo Trese, mentioned these remembrances of his youth:

> There is the memory of Dad, leading the family Rosary. I do not know why the big base-burner in the living room should constantly intrude itself into this image from the past; but there we knelt, stooped over our chairs, while the blue anthracite flames flickered through the windows of the stove. And religion became forever a manly thing, as quiet, hardworking Dad, told the mysteries and led the beads.

There are, of course, different ways of praying the Rosary. Many prefer to walk while reciting the prayers, in order to keep their brain active and alert. What matters most is to truly communicate with the supernatural world, in an exercise of faith and love. Saint Pope John XXIII is said to have remarked in that regard, "There are different kinds of rosaries: dawn rosaries and evening rosaries, alert rosaries and sleepy rosaries, but the worst kind of all is the one that is not prayed."

Pope Paul VI said,

> Your rosary is a stairway, you ascend it together, step by step, approaching our Lady, which means approaching Christ. This is one of the characteristics of the rosary, the most important and the most beautiful of all: it is a devotion which leads us to Christ through His Blessed Mother. Christ is the goal of this lengthy and repeated invocation

of Mary. We speak to Mary so as to reach Christ. She brought Him into the world; she is the mother of the Lord. And she brings us to Him if we are devoted to her.[78]

Spiritual Reading

Continuing with our daily adventure, the day is now far advanced, and if you have not done it earlier in the day (which it is very often the best thing to do), you might still want to do something very important for your soul.

It is something that could be done at home, although at times also at work, outside office hours. It consists in reading from the New Testament for a few minutes and from another spiritual book, all in all for about fifteen minutes.

This practice constitutes another contact with the invisible supernatural world, for the Holy Spirit is the principal Author of the Bible. St. Josemaría gives this advice concerning the practice of reading the Gospels: "If you wish to get close to our Lord through the pages of the Gospels, I always recommend that you try to enter in on the scene taking part as just one more person there."[79]

It is much better to read only a few lines of the New Testament intensely, that is, trying to get some message out of it, than to read many pages without being able to tell what we have read afterwards.

----

[78] Pope Paul VI, *Discourse*, Oct. 10, 1964.
[79] Josemaría Escrivá, *Friends of God* (Manila: Sinag-tala Publishers, 2000), no. 222.

If the other book for spiritual reading—aside from the New Testament—is well chosen, it will contain some sparks of the Light emanating from the concealed Truth. To be well-chosen means that the reader has made sure that it is a book faithful to the teachings of the Church (*Magisterium*), and is suitable for his or her spiritual life. It will often mean, therefore, that it is a book recommended or approved by the spiritual director.

If prayer is the flame of the sanctuary lamp as explained by St. Francis de Sales, then spiritual reading is the oil that feeds it.

Referring to the practice of meditation, Eugene Boyland observes, "One reason why so many fail at mental prayer is that they are trying to make a fire without fuel—they have given up regular spiritual reading."[80] It is important to devote time to this spiritual exercise.

Now, books land into a home in a variety of ways—purchases, gifts, lent by a friend, etc. It is not a matter of reading anything available, but what is truly helpful for our spiritual growth, and to be able to help others in their spiritual challenges.

St. Josemaría tells us, "Don't neglect spiritual reading. Reading has made many saints."[81] This statement holds a great truth. Unfortunately, however, it is also true that reading has confused and distorted the minds of people who read books indiscriminately.

For this reason he added, "Don't buy them without the advice from a Catholic who has real

[80] Eugene Boyland, O.C.R., *The Spiritual Life of a Priest* (Maryland: The Newman Press, 1961), 17.
[81] *The Way*, no. 116.

knowledge and discernment. It's so easy to buy something useless or harmful. How often a man thinks he is carrying a book under his arm, and it turns out to be a load of trash!"[82]

We are getting news and all kinds of information in abundance from different sources. We are bombarded with commercial messages all the time. In contrast, we very seldom hear anything about God and the supernatural realities. Our mind needs to be nourished with something better than earthly things. We need a few minutes of spiritual reading every day, for "man does not live on bread alone."

In order to explain how useful spiritual reading is for the spiritual life, St. Josemaría tells us, "By reading . . . I build up a store of fuel. It seems a lifeless pile, but I often find that my mind spontaneously draws from it material which fills my prayer with life and inflames my thanksgiving after communion."[83]

Naturally, to be careful about selecting books for reading is perfectly compatible with having interest for culture.

> The Christian affirms the same author must have a hunger to know. Everything, from the most abstract knowledge to manual techniques, can and should lead to God. For there is no human undertaking which cannot be sanctified, which cannot be an opportunity to sanctify ourselves and to cooperate with God in the sanctification of the people with whom we work. The light

---

[82] Ibid., no. 339.
[83] *The Way*, no. 213.

of the followers of Jesus Christ should not be hidden in the depths of some valley, but should be placed on the mountain peak, so that they may see your good works and give glory to your Father in heaven.[84]

In other words, spiritual reading is important not only for our own spiritual development, but also for the help we are to give to those we manage to reach in our apostolic efforts. The love of our neighbor, which stems from our love of God, impels us to be capable to light up the minds and enkindle the hearts of those near us with the light of the Gospel, and no one can give what he does not have.

In our spiritual life and in our apostolate, we need to form and address the mind, the will, and the heart. This is why we should read sound spiritual books that belong to these different categories. It might be good to alternate them. For instance, after reading a doctrinal book, like the *Compendium of the Catholic Church*, it could be ideal to read *Friends of God* by St. Josemaría Escrivá, which is more ascetical in content; and afterward a book like *Man the Saint* by Jesus Urteaga, written with youthful passion; or *Jesus as Friend* by Salvatore Canals, which has a very serene prose with much spiritual drive. Depending on our own particular circumstances, we will need books that largely address the mind or the will.

Debunking the idea that the Church is needlessly "afraid" of ideas—that all philosophical and moral positions are essentially harmless, the well-known Prof. James Stenson explains,

---

[84] Mt 5:16; Josemaría Escrivá, *Christ is Passing By*, no. 10.

To the Church, a person's loss of grace, along with the faith that might lead him back to it, is an unimaginably tragic disaster. No physical calamity, no merely temporal suffering can compare with this loss. . . .

The Church has seen, time and again in history, that ideas can have profound and far reaching consequences. It has witnessed how doctrines contrary to Christian belief have led to people's personal misery and even to social catastrophe . . . . For generations, the Church has seen people embrace doctrinal aberrations to rationalize and justify their appetites, especially in sexual morality and the drive for power.[85]

We should, therefore, learn how to choose the books we read by paying attention to our mother, the Church. She gives ecclesiastical approvals, the *Nihil Obstat* and the *Imprimatur,* to the editions of the Bible, and to other doctrinal books touching on faith and morals for our own benefit and guidance.

It is not always easy to be faithful to the practice of daily spiritual reading. Excuses such as the lack of time or the urgency of other things seemingly more important often crop up. It is, again, a matter of faith. The things of God should be given priority. For that, readiness to exert the necessary effort is required. St. Josemaría has described well the usual inner struggle involved in fulfilling the plan of life:

If you are struggling, and even more if you are really struggling, you should not be

---

[85] James B. Stenson, *Reading: Learning To Choose* (London and New York: Scepter Publishers, 1984), 19-21.

surprised at feeling tired or at times having to go against the grain, without any spiritual or human consolation. See what someone wrote to me some time ago, and which I kept for those who naively consider that grace does away with nature, "Father, for a few days now I have been feeling tremendously lazy and lacking in enthusiasm for fulfilling the plan of life. I have to force myself to do everything, and I have very little taste for it. Pray for me so that this crisis may pass, for it makes me suffer a lot to think it could make me turn from my way."

I answer only: did you not know that Love demands sacrifice?[86]

It is worthwhile to conquer ourselves in order to nourish our soul with the light of the Gospel. It will give us peace and strength to face the daily challenges of life.

Looking Inside Our Soul While Facing God

You are now about to end the day. Your mind turns towards the unseen World, *"Where the true joys are found."* First of all, you look at the nucleus of the *Cloud of Witnesses* of your life, the Triune God, and ask the Holy Spirit to illumine you in order to answer three simple questions that St. Josemaría recommended in some cases: *Lord, what have I done*

----

[86] Cf. *Furrow*, no. 149.

today that has displeased You? What have I done that has pleased You? What can I do better tomorrow? To this effect, a specific and firm resolution will be very helpful.

The discovery of failures leads to the most important part of this brief exercise: an act of sincere *sorrow of love*, which is very different from an act of *sorrow of pride* that is motivated by the disappointment of not seeing oneself as perfect as one would wish to be.

Venerable Fulton Sheen was fond of saying that self-examination must be done in the presence of God, for we must compare ourselves not with our neighbor, nor with our subjective ideal, but with Christ.

The examination of conscience allows us to know our strengths better, and in this way to improve our life. It helps us to detect whatever separates us from God or affects our intimacy with Jesus Christ.

St. Josemaría writes, "Examination of conscience. A daily task. Book keeping—never neglected by anyone in business. And is there any business worth more than that of eternal life?"[87]

The realization of good things done during the day should not be a reason to be complacent, rather, it should be a motive of thanksgiving to the Almighty without whom we can do nothing.

This is a well-known truism of Thales of Miletus: "The most difficult thing is to know oneself, the easiest is to criticize others."

If we do the examination of conscience well, we will obtain from the Lord self-knowledge, contrition

---

[87] *The Way*, no. 235.

for our sins, abandonment in God's will, and resolutions. We will avoid falling into lukewarmness this way.

The setting of one or two goals for the following day, that could be written down, is very helpful in our quest to improve in our daily struggle and move ahead in our attempt to reach sanctity to which we are all called, as St. Josemaría Escrivá hammered in his preaching since 1928, and which Vatican II solemnly proclaimed in 1965.

This brief examination of conscience is a good preparation for the Sacrament of Reconciliation that we need to receive immediately, if we were to commit a mortal sin; and also, on a regular basis, weekly, fortnightly, or at least monthly, in order to make swift progress in our spiritual life.

Calling It a Day

Finally, it is now time to rest. Still, before that, a lifting of the mind and heart to the silent supernatural world comes in handy in the form of three Hail Marys asking Our Lady for holy purity, for oneself, and for everybody else. The very last thing that could be done is to make the sign of the Cross and sprinkle a couple of drops of holy water on the bed to drive Satan away. St. Teresa of Jesus affirmed: "I know by frequent experience that there is nothing which puts the devil to flight like holy water."[88]

---

[88] St. Teresa of Jesus, *The Life of St. Teresa of Jesus* (London: Tomas Baker, 1904; New York: Doubleday-Image Book, 1960), 198.

Looking back at the day that has passed, we see that with God's help, it has been a happy day lived with both feet well-grounded on this earth, and yet ever in touch with the supernatural Audience. It has been, therefore, a great day, a day worth living!

As a whole, it has been a day inspired by pieces of advice mostly coming from St. Josemaría Escrivá, the founder of Opus Dei. Definitely, it has been a joyful day, lived while holding dual citizenship in heaven and on earth, loving passionately the concealed Friend and also ardently loving the world.

Something for Every Day of the Week

As St. Josemaría suggested, our contact with the invisible Audience could be very well-seasoned if we place a particular emphasis on each day of the week. For instance, on **Mondays,** it would be a good idea to remember often the blessed souls in Purgatory. They certainly belong to the silent realm beyond the *barrier* that separates us from the *other side*. However, they are blessed, for the grace of God is with them. They are becoming more and more inflamed with the love of God and in union with Him, and they can interact with us, thanks to the Communion of Saints, which comprises communication.

Accordingly, when we pass in front of a cemetery, when we read an obituary, or when we come across a funeral procession, it would occur to us spontaneously to say a prayer for "My good friends, the souls in purgatory."[89]

I recall asking someone once, who was quite a joker, what he does when he passes by a cemetery. His answer was quick: "Well, I just press down the accelerator!"

We certainly could do better than that, by saying a short prayer like: "Lord, grant them eternal life! May they rest in peace!"

Above all, it would be an excellent idea to remember these *friends of ours*, the souls in Purgatory, in our times of prayer and at the Holy Mass, which is always offered "for the living *and the dead.*"

Tuesdays, on the other hand, could be especially devoted to fostering a close relationship with our Guardian Angel. Perhaps, you would like to call him fondly with some name. It might help you to address him trustfully. It is in line with what St. Josemaría tells us: "Have confidence in your Guardian Angel. Treat him as a very dear friend—that's what he is—and he will do a thousand services for you in the ordinary affairs of each day."[90] And he adds, "If you would remember the presence of your Guardian Angel and those of your neighbors, you would avoid many of the foolish things you let slip into your conversation."[91]

Moreover, on this same day, you might want to remember more often that powerful angelic protector the Lord has given us, as we take the Test and Game of our earthly sojourn, in order to counteract

---

[89] Cf. *The Way*, no. 571.
[90] Ibid., no. 562.
[91] Ibid., no. 564.

the diabolic influence felt in our midst. It may help you to say:

> St. Michael the Archangel, defend us in battle. Be our defense against the wickedness and snares of the devil. May God rebuke him, we humbly pray and do you, O Prince of the heavenly hosts, by the power of God, thrust into hell Satan, and the evil spirits who prowl about the world seeking the ruin of souls. Amen.

You may also want to say more often the prayer you perhaps learned when you were still a little kid: *Angel of God, my guardian dear, to whom His love commits me here, ever this day/night be at my side, to light and guard, to rule and guide. Amen.*

Wednesdays could be the days in which we try to communicate more often and more intensely with St. Joseph. He is not only the faithful foster father of our Lord Jesus Christ, the virginal spouse of the Virgin Mary, the prudent head and provider of the lovely household of Nazareth, but also the model of workers, the master of prayer and interior life, the patron of the dying (for he was, most likely, fortunate enough to have Jesus and Mary at his side at the moment of his death), and also the Patron of the Universal Church.

By this last title, we are reminded that St. Joseph is linked personally and truly with each human being. He belongs to the *silent and supernatural world*. But this does not mean that he is like a ghost. No, he is very real and he is interested in all of us, for Jesus—whom he helped in His redemptive work— shed His Blood for all mankind. He is truly a most loving father to everyone. This is how St. Josemaría puts it: "St. Joseph, a father to Christ, is also your father and your lord. Have recourse to him."[92]

Also on Wednesdays, we could make it a point to invoke St. Joseph for all our needs. At prayer time, we could address him confidently, paying special attention to him. In addition, we could ask him to teach us how to deal and communicate properly with our Lord and our Blessed Mother.

Thursdays are forever linked to the Holy Eucharist, for it was on a Thursday that our Lord, during the Last Supper, instituted it. It might be a good idea to devote this day to meditate and converse with the Persons of the veiled Audience about this great Mystery of Faith.

This is how St. Matthew, inspired by the Holy Spirit, recorded for us the institution of the Eucharist:

> Now as they were eating, Jesus took bread, and blessed, and broke it, and gave it to the disciples and said, "Take, eat; this is my body." And he took a cup, and when he had given thanks he gave it to them, saying, "Drink of it, all of you; for this is my blood of the new covenant, which is poured out for many for the forgiveness of sins."[93]

It was the farewell supper that linked the old and the new covenants, in order that the following day would be sealed on the Cross, with the precious blood of our Lord.

---

92 *The Way*, no. 559.
93 Mt 26: 26-28

It is appropriate, therefore, to do all we can to make every Thursday a Eucharistic day. We could begin by attending Holy Mass, even if we are not yet able to do so on the other weekdays. It is a great thing to be present at the re-presentation of the sacrifice of Calvary and to worthily receive the Bread of Life on a day which is not a holy day of obligation. Under these circumstances, we enjoy the additional and personal assurance that we attend the Holy Mass, not out of any fear or requirement, but out of pure and free love.

Still on Thursdays, we could make it a point to bring to our prayer this great mystery of love, and not to fail in visiting our Lord in the Blessed Sacrament, the silent, and often lonely Guest of countless Catholic churches and chapels.

In addition, we could endeavor to multiply the expression of our eagerness to receive Him sacramentally, by reciting Spiritual Communions throughout the day. Many have found it helpful to use one St. Josemaría learned when he was preparing for his first Communion: "I wish, Lord, to receive you with the purity, humility and devotion with which your most holy mother received you, with the spirit and fervor of the saints."

On **Fridays**, the memory of Mount Calvary looms high. It was on a Friday when Jesus was hung on a cross for our salvation. It would be a great pity if we were so immersed in our earthly pursuits that such remembrance would not mean anything to us. Therefore, we will do well in making an effort to recall it throughout the day. Without doubt, the best moment for that will be in the Sacrifice of the Mass that we attend. There we find ourselves at Golgotha, with the same High Priest, the same Victim, and the same intention Jesus Christ had at that time. We get a glimpse of how this is possible on account of the fact that He, the eternal Logos (the Second Person of the Blessed Trinity), always lives—as God—in eternity, that is, outside the constraints of time and space.

If it is truly compatible with our professional and family duties, it would be an excellent thing to recite on Fridays, the Way of the Cross, a practice that our mother the Church has enriched with generous indulgences. This is how St. Josemaría puts it:

> The Way of the Cross. Here indeed is a strong and fruitful devotion! May you make it a habit to go over those fourteen points of our Lord's Passion and Death each Friday. I assure you that you'll gain strength for the whole week.[94]

To that, Blessed Alvaro del Portillo added, "The Way of the Cross is not a sad devotion. Msgr. Escrivá taught many times that Christian joy has its roots in the shape of a cross. If the Passion of Christ is a way of pain, it is also a path of hope leading to certain victory."[95]

Saturdays have always been linked to our Blessed Mother Mary. Christians have not forgotten that sorrowful Saturday, when the body of Jesus Christ laid in the tomb, and Mary inspired confidence to the disciples and provided them with the

---

[94] *The Way*, no. 556.
[95] Alvaro del Portillo, Foreword to *The Way of the Cross* by Josemaría Escrivá (London: Scepter, 1982), 13.

great support of her unshakable faith. At the darkest hour, Mary was truly the hope of the Christians. For this reason, over the centuries, Saturday has been a day devoted to Our Lady.

It would be an excellent idea to make every Saturday a Marian day. We could begin by paying special attention to her when we make our Morning Offering and address the Triune God and His entourage. She is the Queen of Heaven, that is, the most important person in our Lord's retinue. After God comes Mary, and she deserves our special attention. Accordingly, after offering our entire day to the Almighty, we might want to speak filially to the Virgin Mary, asking her protection during the day.

There is an ancient and very well-known prayer, the *Memorare*, that Christians have prayed countless times, and it comes to us from St. Bernard of Clairvaux (+1153), a Doctor of the Church, who was very much in love with Mary. It would be a good thing to say it often on Saturdays. It goes:

> Remember, O most gracious Virgin Mary, that never was it known that anyone who fled to your protection, implored your help or sought your intercession, was left unaided. Inspired by this confidence, I fly unto you, O Virgin of virgins, my Mother. To you I come, before you I stand, sinful and sorrowful. O Mother of the Word incarnate, despise not my petitions, but, in your mercy, hear and answer me. Amen.

In addition, since Saturdays are devoted to Our Lady, it would be fitting to pray with more intensity all our Marian devotions, such as the Holy Rosary. This is what Pope Pius XII said about it:

> What a sweet and most pleasing spectacle to God when, at eventide, the Christian home resounds with repeated praises in honor of the august Queen of heaven! Then the recitation of the Rosary reunites the parents and their children who return from their daily work and brings them together before the image of the Virgin in an admirable union of hearts. It unites them piously with those absent and with the dead.[96]

Furthermore, Saint Pope John XXIII called it "the most excellent meditated prayer."[97] The popes have wholeheartedly recommended the Holy Rosary and have enriched it with indulgences.

It is also very appropriate to recite or sing a Hail Holy Queen every Saturday in her honor. It is an ancient and very beautiful prayer that surely will please our Blessed Mother. As in the Hail Mary, we remind the Virgin Mary of her splendid titles, most especially of her condition as Queen, and we end humbly, asking her help for us who are still "in this our exile." It is a prayer that is bound to touch her Immaculate Heart.

Through Sister Lucia of Fatima, Our Lady has also requested that we observe with particular devotion the first Saturday of each month: attending Holy Mass, receiving worthy Communion of reparation

---

[96] Pope Pius XII, Encyclical *Ad Apostolorum Principis*, June 29, 1958, no. 10.

[97] John XXIII, Encyclical on the Rosary *Grata Recordatio*, Sep. 26, 1959.

for sins, and praying the Rosary in honor of her Immaculate Heart for five consecutive Saturdays. It might be a good idea to live this devotion every first Saturday of the month.

In line with this advice that comes from Our Lady herself, it would be a praiseworthy resolution to dedicate every first Saturday to live and propagate among our friends the love for the Immaculate Heart of Mary, and to offer atonement for the sins that are committed all over the world.

Finally, on **Sundays**, in addition to the weekly commemoration of the Resurrection of Our Lord, we could devote them to honoring, in a special way, the Blessed Trinity, which is at the very core and summit of the *Company of Witnesses* of our lives. The *Catechism of the Catholic Church* calls the mystery of the Most Holy Trinity "the central mystery of the Christian faith and life."[98]

This great mystery should not only occupy first position at the speculative level, it should also be so at the practical level of the lives of Christians. A good contribution to this is making every Sunday a special *Trinitarian day.*

Still on Sundays, whenever making the sign of the Cross is called for, we could strive to do it in such a way that we really mean what we are saying: *"In the name of the Father, and of the Son, and of the Holy Spirit!"* Furthermore, we could bring to our mental prayer this great mystery of our faith, taking it as the topic of meditation for a few minutes and, perhaps, occasionally, we might find it useful to use

---

[98] *Catechism of the Catholic Church*, no. 234.

the words of the *Te Deum*, the *Angelic Trisagion*, or the *Athanasian Creed*.

During Sundays, while going from one occupation to another, we might find it helpful to repeat some aspiration as, for instance: *"Glory be to the Father, to the Son, to the Holy Spirit!"* or this one that St. Josemaría said and recommended a great deal: *"Hail Mary, daughter of God the Father, Hail Mary, mother of God the Son, Hail Mary, spouse of God the Holy Spirit, more than you only God!"*

Frequent Confession

A mong the practices recommended by the unanimous and constant Catholic Tradition, the Sacrament of Reconciliation holds pride of place. Saints, doctors of the Church, popes, and bishops have always advised the frequent reception of this sacrament. Furthermore, those who have founded new institutions within the Church for the purpose of promoting, among other goals, the sanctification of its members, have persistently established the weekly—or at least very frequent reception—of this sacrament of joy and peace we call confession. The reason is clear: It was established by Jesus Christ as a sacrament, a channel of grace, of reconciliation with God and the Church, and a powerful means for spiritual growth.

Confession is there not only to forgive sins and give sanctifying grace if it was lost. It also increases this grace. It is instrumental in helping and enriching the soul in the form of sacramental grace and actual graces that allow us to have more strength to overcome temptations and strive for virtue. Confession makes us humbler. It is, therefore, a great means for spiritual progress. In consequence, the more a soul desires to be united to God, the more it wishes to receive the Sacrament of Penance. This sacrament is wholly necessary for the forgiveness of grave sins. The act of perfect contrition forgives mortal sins only if it is accompanied by a desire to receive the Sacrament of Reconciliation.

The precept of going to confession once a year, if we had any mortal sin, is a mere **minimum**. It aims to ensure that we do not despise the opportunity of reconciliation that Jesus Christ offers to us through His Church. But, if we take seriously the words from Sacred Scripture which are addressed to every one: "This is the will of God, your sanctification,"[99] then, the need for more frequent confession becomes crystal clear.

Some persons are hesitant to go to confession, for they feel that their sins are too many and too grievous. They are to bear in mind this passage from St. Luke:

> And the Pharisees and their Scribes were grumbling, saying to his disciples, "Why do you eat and drink with publicans and sinners?" And Jesus answered and said to them, "It is not the healthy who need a physician, but they who are sick. I have not come to call the just, but sinners to repentance."[100]

---

[99] 1 Thess 4:3.
[100] Lk 5:31-32.

Our Lord is "rich in mercy" to an amazing degree. St. Josemaría puts it this way:

> Consider what depths of mercy lie in the Justice of God! For, according to human justice, he who pleads guilty is punished, but in the divine court, he is pardoned. Blessed be the holy sacrament of Penance![101]

Moreover, in order to stress this point, Jesus Himself said, "I tell you, there will be more joy in heaven over one sinner who repents than over ninety-nine righteous who do not need repentance."[102] This text shows how grateful we should be for His immense mercy every time we receive the Sacrament of Reconciliation.

In confession, it is essential to be repentant of having committed sins. It is not enough to regret having done something wrong, or to be eager to leave its memory behind. We ought to be truly determined not to do it anymore. Moreover, the reason for this repentance should be the love of God. He is the one Who is most importantly offended. Emotional sensations and tears are welcome, if sincere, but not at all necessary.

Aside from the immense supernatural advantages of frequent confession, there are a number of human returns. Raphael Bonelli, an Austrian psychiatrist, says,

> Normally, a person who confesses regularly obtains a high knowledge of himself, or herself. The reason is that he or she develops the capacity to question himself, or

---

[101] *The Way*, no. 309.
[102] Lk 15:7.

herself, and to pass judgment on his or her emotions, feelings, passions and actions. Such a person acquires the aptitude to prioritize the power of reflection over a passing sensation, and does not perceive his or her own actions as events bound to destiny, but as something to submit to a rational judgment. This leads to a healthy consciousness of oneself, rooted in one's condition as a son or daughter of God. Ultimately, it translates itself into an attitude of deep gratitude to a merciful God, who forgives sins. Such persons are able to forgive more easily other individuals who have injured them. Moreover, they live more peacefully and more cheerfully.[103]

Spiritual Guidance

Spiritual direction stands side by side with frequent confession. In line with the entire Catholic Tradition, St. Josemaría recommends it wholeheartedly:

> It's good for you to know this doctrine, which is always sound: your own spirit is a bad advisor, a poor pilot to steer your soul through the squalls and storms and across the reefs of the interior life.

[103] Raphael Bonelli, *Palabra* (Madrid: Ediciones Palabra, July 2012), no. 589.

That's why it is the Will of God that the command of the ship be entrusted to a master who, with his light and knowledge, can guide us to a safe port.[104]

He further explains the need for spiritual direction, saying: "You wouldn't think of building a good house to live on earth without an architect. How can you ever hope, without a director, to build the castle of your sanctification in order to live forever in heaven?"[105]

It can also be compared to coaching in sports, for the Christian life is a supernatural test that requires training and guidance. It is a recognized fact in the world of sports that having a good coach often spells the difference between victory and defeat for a given team or player.

Undoubtedly, the principal director of each soul is the Holy Spirit. We need to listen to Him and follow His promptings with docility. It is also His will that we obediently follow the advice given to us by His representative who guides us in spiritual matters and who acts like an instrument of the veiled Spirit.

Accordingly, it is wise to meditate afterwards on the advice we have received in our personal prayer, and to find a way to put it into practice, with the certainty that it is the will of God for us.

It is a great thing to have someone who has a special help from God to whom we can tell, with freedom, our ups and downs, our joys and sorrows, in order to receive some comfort or some

---

[104] *The Way*, no. 59.
[105] Ibid., no. 60.

encouragement. Above all, it is great because it is a supernatural means, highly recommended by the Church to become closer to God.

We are to go punctually to spiritual direction with the humility of a child, with eagerness to be known as we really are, with the desire to be helped in our spiritual struggle; thus, making it easy for whoever guides our soul to demand more from us, as well as pointing out, without hesitation, whatever needs to be mentioned.

It follows from the considerations above that the virtue of sincerity is very important for an effective spiritual direction. St. Josemaría says, "Anyone who hides a temptation from his director shares a secret with the devil. He has become a friend of the enemy."[106] And he adds: "If you are sincere with God, with your director, and your fellowmen, I shall be certain of your perseverance."[107]

Upon entrusting the direction of our soul to a qualified person, we do not in any way lose our freedom, responsibility, and initiative. This is similar to how a pilot of a commercial plane does not lack freedom when he pays much attention to what is said from the control tower. He trusts the advice given, and knows that it is for his own good as well as for the good of many others. No pilot thinks that his freedom is restricted by the control tower, for it is clear to him that he is in control of the plane, and that he has to assume the consequent responsibility.

---

[106] *Furrow*, no. 323.
[107] Ibid., no. 325.

Monthly

No matter how busy we are, it is very good to take some time out once a month to further our spiritual life. It is a matter of being with our Lord in more familiar terms than usual and to deepen our knowledge and implementation of the Christian Faith.

It is a golden opportunity to have a lengthier contact with our Lord and to genuinely examine our conscience.

It is a little break from our usual daily activities, in order to be *in silence with God* and to be closer to Him. When the time for our monthly recollection comes, we are to give preference to this opportunity to be with our Lord—often facing the tabernacle—over other temporal concerns.

The purpose of the day of recollection is to improve our spiritual formation and to immerse ourselves more deeply in God. Hence, it would not be right to limit ourselves to listening to a series of meditations and talks, as if they constituted an academic affair. They are not mere classes or lectures. They are supposed to help us grow in our interior life.

It is not so much a matter of always hearing new things, in what has been termed as *neolatria* (worshipping novelty), but digging deeper and deeper into the inexhaustible Christian message, applying it to ourselves and sharing it with others. The monthly recollection, in fact, is an excellent occasion to invite friends to come to know our Lord and His teachings better. When they come for the first time, it is a matter of *playing host* by showing them around, introducing them to others, and explaining to them the goal and the events of the activity.

Yearly

*A*s it is commonly known, it is very helpful to set aside, once a year, a few days to commune with God, to grow in the interior life and develop our contemplative spirit. It also helps us to review our spiritual struggles of the previous months and to come up with a few realistic resolutions.

Many recognize the importance of an annual check-up for our bodily health. Should we not value our spiritual health even more?

It is a period dedicated entirely to our Lord. The observance of silence facilitates our inner conversation with the withdrawn God. Noise is an obstacle we are to avoid in a retreat.

A retreat provides an occasion to leave behind our daily concerns, leaving them in God's hands, and to focus our attention on the most important matters in our lives.

Always

℞ elating with our veiled God and very loving Father is something that has to be done not daily or weekly, but always. That is, to maintain the **presence of God**. It consists in being aware that He is alive and looking lovingly at us. It amounts to removing the veil that covers the hidden Father.

Perhaps, we recall very fondly instances in our lives in which we have perceived God's presence vividly. They are no more than subjective experiences, and thus, they lack objective value. Nevertheless, for us, for our own personal pilgrimage of faith, they are very valuable.

In order to habitually have presence of God, we are to slow down a bit to avoid being always too much in a hurry. We are to ponder things and give importance to what is truly important. It is equally necessary to have enough self-dominion to reject energetically frivolous thoughts and images that might invade our mind, our imagination, and our memory. It is also important to fill our heart with aspirations that express the supernatural love we have in our heart. That is, to carry a conversation with the Persons of the veiled supernatural world. All this requires that we bear ever in mind that there is, as it were, a *one-way mirror* between us and God, and the other world. He sees us perfectly, but we do not see Him.

St. Josemaría writes:

It's necessary to be convinced that God is always near us. Too often we live as though Our Lord were somewhere far off—where the stars shine. We fail to realize that He is also by our side—always.

For He is a loving Father. He loves each one of us more than all the mothers in the world can love their children, helping us, blessing . . . and forgiving.[108]

When St. Josemaría was working on the documents for the canonical approvals of the Work, he had on his table a green piece of glass that had been used on an electric post as an insulator. Cables carrying electric current had been placed around it. The founder of Opus Dei reflected on this and concluded that he did not want to be an obstacle to the transmission of supernatural grace. That piece of cheap glass helped him ask Jesus, time and again, never to be an insulator of grace, but a good conductor of spiritual energy. On his working table, under a round piece of crystal, he kept the following inscriptions:

Sufre, si quieres gozar
(Suffer, if you want to enjoy)

Baja, si quieres subir
(Come down, if you want to go up)

Pierde, si quieres ganar
(Lose, if you want to win)

Muere, si quieres vivir
(Die, if you want to live)

I have a small picture of the founder of Opus Dei where, in May 1958, he had written: *Semper ut*

---

108 *The Way*, no. 267.

iumentum! (Always like a donkey!) It was an expression of his fondness for this little animal on account of its perseverance, hard work, austerity, and humility. He had a similar fondness for ducks, about which he said with good humor, "I like the fact that ducks learn to swim by swimming." The sight of these animals were good aids in maintaining his presence of God.

On his working desk in a house on Diego de Leon Street in Madrid, and later in Rome, the founder of Opus Dei had a globe, which he liked to turn around to help him pray for the apostolate carried out by his daughters and sons all over the five continents.

For bookmarks, he used strips of paper with the phrase: *Ure Sancte Spiritus!* (Inflame with the fire of the Holy Spirit) written in his bold handwriting.[109]

St. Josemaría made many suggestions for "human devices" like:

> Before you start working, place a crucifix on your desk or beside the tools you work with. From time to time glance at it. . . . When tiredness creeps in, your eyes will go towards Jesus, and you will find new strength to continue with your task.

> For that crucifix is more than a picture of someone you love—parents, children, wife, sweetheart . . . He is everything: your father, your brother, your friend, your God, the very love of your loves.[110]

It is the same idea conveyed in a touching point of his book, *The Way*:

---

[109] *The Forge*, no. 923.
[110] *The Way of the Cross*, no. 97.

You ask me, "Why that wooden Cross?" And I quote from a letter: "As I raise my eyes from the microscope, my sight comes to rest on the Cross—black and empty. That Cross without a Corpus is a symbol; it has a meaning others won't see. And I, tired out and on the point of abandoning my work, once again bring my eyes close to the lens and continue. For that lonely Cross is calling for a pair of shoulders to bear it."[111]

It is as striking as this point in *Furrow:*

You are writing to me in the kitchen, by the stove. It is early afternoon. It is cold. By your side, your youngest sister—the last one to discover the divine folly of living her Christian vocation to the full—is peeling potatoes. To all appearances, you think her work is the same as before. And yet, what a difference there is!

It is true: before she *only* peeled potatoes, now, she is sanctifying herself peeling potatoes.[112]

The Lord, who is pleased with the incense offered to Him during a solemn liturgical ceremony is also pleased with the toil offered in countless settings in the world of labor, manual or intellectual, when it is offered to Him as a gift to the Father, in union with the Son, with the help of the Holy Spirit. In this manner, it becomes an act of "worship" that has

---

[111] *The Way*, no. 277.
[112] *Furrow*, no. 498.

a co-redeeming value: through Him, with Him, and in Him!

St. Josemaría advises this for all moments:

> Be convinced, my child, that God has a right to ask us: Are you thinking about me? Are you aware of me? Do you look at me as your support? Do you seek me as the Light of your life, as your shield . . . as your all?
>
> Renew, then, this resolution: In times the world calls good, I will cry out: "Lord!" In times it calls bad, again I will cry: "Lord!"[113]

He adds, "Ask yourself many times during the day: Am I doing at this moment what I ought to be doing?"[114] And for the occasions in which things seem to go well,

> Have you seen the gratitude of little children? Imitate them, saying to Jesus when things are favorable and when they aren't, "How good you are! How good!"[115]

Lastly, as we try to find the covered God, we find Him reflected in our fellowmen; and we are guided by the Gospels that show how Jesus identified Himself with the neighbor: "Whatever you do to the least one among you, you did it for Me."[116]

The realization that the veiled God is our Father who loves us more than all the most loving fathers on this earth put together is a most fundamental and consoling truth. It should have a number of

---

[113] *The Forge*, no. 506.
[114] *The Way*, no. 772.
[115] Ibid., no. 894.
[116] Mt 25:40.

manifestations stemming from what we could call a **"sense of divine filiation."** Examples of this could be: the attentive and unhurried recitation of the Lord's Prayer, paying special attention to the words, "Our Father"; bringing to our prayer, as a frequent topic of meditation, the great truth of being adopted children of God; addressing our veiled Lord with words such as, "Hi, Daddy!" *(Abba, Pater!);* to value very much and to celebrate the anniversary of our Baptism, for on that day we became children of God and heirs of heaven. Heirs, that is, of the treasures Jesus Christ has earned for us with His Blood.

The sheltered God is only so in order to enable us to take with all freedom the great test of faith which is our life. Actually, He is eager to be with us; He delights being among us. He calls us and comes to us, while remaining a withdrawn Lord only for the sake of the Game and Test we are taking.

Acts of thanksgiving for the favors received from His invisible Hand should be done more frequently. Practice thanksgiving for everything, for, as St. Paul teaches: *"For those who love God, all things work together unto good."*[117] Hence, we are to be thankful for those things that are obviously good, and for those which are not so, if permitted by Him. Moreover, we are to be grateful for the many blessings we have received even though we are not aware of them.

Considering that the silent God is offended without pause all over the world, it is our duty to offer expiation for sins. For instance, the prayer taught by the Angel to the little shepherds of Fatima

---

[117] Rom 8:28.

includes this moving line: "My God, I believe, I adore, I hope, and I love You. I ask pardon for all those who do not believe, do not adore, do not hope, and do not love You."

In a similar vein, St. Josemaría says: "Don't be so blind or so thoughtless that you fail to say at least an ejaculation to Mary Immaculate, whenever you go past a place where you know Christ is being offended."[118]

Those above are instances of *acts of atonement* for the many sins committed against the Lord all over the world (sadly an enormous amount every minute). In the year 2011, the National Center for Victims of Crime reported that in the USA:

- One child dies from abuse or neglect every 5 hours
- One person is murdered every 35 minutes
- One person is robbed every 1.3 minutes
- One person is raped or sexually assaulted every 4.2 minutes
- One person is killed in an alcohol-related traffic crash every 48.5 minutes.

This is a partial account of the so-called American "crime clock." It is an appalling statistical report of crimes committed every day, every hour, every minute in the USA. It is sobering to think that God, the silent Examiner, is continuously witnessing many more sins perpetrated all over the world, including many that are committed internally and therefore undetectable, but are real offenses to Him. We get easily distracted, but He never does;

---

[118] Cf. *The Way*, no. 269.

He perceives absolutely everything and Jesus Christ paid for it on Calvary with His Blood.

We are to offer some token expiation for sins, knowing that many of them are atrocious. Our desire to atone for sins should extend first to our own, and then, to all those committed since the beginning of mankind and to all those that will be perpetrated till the end of time. In other words, to all the offenses directed to our loving Lord in the past, present, and future. St. Josemaría says,

> We want to offer our life, our unstinting dedication, in expiation for our sins; for the sins of all men, our brothers; for the sins committed at all times, and for those that will be committed until the end of time. Above all, for the Catholics, for God's chosen ones who do not respond, those who betray the special love God our Lord has bestowed on them.
>
> **To be second to none in loving**; to win all souls for Christ; to offer abundant reparation for the offenses committed against the most Sacred Heart of Jesus: these are our ambitions.[119]

Furthermore, it is always a good time for *aspirations* that could be compared to darts that spring from the mind and heart and might reach the mouth. They are short and simple ejaculatory prayers that each one might want to compose or select. Some are spontaneous expressions of genuine love for God and the other Persons of the concealed supernatural world. Others are cries for help or expressions

---

[119] St. Josemaría Escrivá, *Letter*, Jan. 9, 1932, 83.

of some other sentiment, like: *Jesus, I love you! Mary, help!* Often, these spontaneous reactions are prompted by the sight of some holy picture or a crucifix that remind us of lofty realities. They respond to a need of our heart and of our human condition.

On those occasions, wherein the mind finds it difficult to communicate with the living God, aspirations come in very handy; they are the little twigs that keep the sacred fire of our life of faith alive.

In addition, frequent, little sacrifices, acts of self-denial or **mortification**, offered as tokens of love for Christ crucified, could not be lacking in a person who wants to co-redeem with the Lord. There is no greater honor than to be permitted to suffer with Christ. St. Josemaría says, "Jesus suffers to carry out the will of the Father. And you, who also want to carry out the most holy Will of God, following the steps of the Master, can you complain if you meet suffering on your way?"[120]

Mortification is our tool to heal the wounds inflicted in our nature by sin. By keeping the body under the control of the soul, we permit God's grace to restore the harmony which sin has managed to destroy.

Judging by the way many people react at the face of pain, they seem to have forgotten that Paradise was lost a long time ago. In this testing ground, in this exile, the veiled Examiner wants us to react properly. The founder of Opus Dei says, "In this life, we must expect the Cross. Those who do not expect the Cross are not Christians, and they will be unable

[120] *The Way*, no. 213.

to avoid their own 'cross,' which will drive them to despair."[121]

Without a Christian vision of things, suffering seems to be something weird and beyond our understanding. And yet, when considered with eyes of faith and with trust in our veiled Father, pain has meaning. It shows us God's Providence. It is a means to purify us by removing the scars due to sins. When needed, it shortens or even cancels our future stay in Purgatory. It also helps us to be humble; that is, realistic, upon experiencing the limitations and the truth of our present human condition. Suffering leads us to be more understanding towards our fellow human beings and unites us more closely with Jesus Christ, giving us the opportunity to co-redeem with Him. Additionally, suffering makes us more useful and fruitful in the immense apostolate done by the Church throughout the world.

Every so often, the Cross of our Savior comes our way without our searching for it. It comes in real circumstances, not imagined. On other instances though, they are not objective; we "invent" them. In both cases we ought to take things well. We are to climb up those steps suggested by St. Josemaría: "to be resigned to the Will of God; to conform to the Will of God, to want the Will of God; to love the Will of God."[122]

In addition to accepting the passive sufferings the veiled Proctor wishes to send us, we are to look for ways of offering to Him tokens of our love in the form of little active sacrifices. These little acts of self-denial will prepare us to take well the

---

[121] *The Forge*, no. 763.
[122] *The Way*, no. 774.

bigger challenges we might meet in life. If we were self-indulgent, however, we would easily fail when big temptations or huge sufferings come our way. The reason is simple: we have become, somehow, like spoiled brats.

Mortification of the Senses

(O)ur senses are like the windows of our soul. It is through them that it gets in contact with the surrounding world, and we want that only good things will reach our soul. Consequently, we need to mortify each one of our senses.

First, the sense of *sight*: "Why should you look around, if you carry 'your world' within you?"[123] "The eyes! Through them much wickedness enters into the soul. How many experiences like David's! If you guard your eyes, you'll be assured of guarding your heart."[124]

We are to be on guard and control our sight, especially when using the Internet, or viewing movies and videos.

Then, our sense of *hearing*: We are also to exert custody over it, preventing it from getting things incompatible with our love for God, and also avoiding, or cutting short, conversations that do not please the Lord and amount to a waste of time.

Similarly, also, our sense of *taste*: We should include "among the ingredients of our meals . . .

---

[123] Ibid., no. 184.
[124] Ibid., no. 183.

that 'most delicious' of ingredients, mortification."[125] As it was advised by St. Josemaría, "To eat a bit less of what we like most, and a bit more of what we like less." "The body must be given a little less than it needs. Otherwise it will turn traitor."[126] And we are also warned that: "Gluttony is the forerunner of impurity."[127]

We are to eat with temperance and drink alcoholic beverages with sobriety. Hence, it is better not to give the body full satisfaction in these things. It is enough to consume what is needed to keep our body healthy and efficient, and no more.

Mortification of the Interior Senses

Interior mortification is important for, as Eugene Boyland says, "No man who always says 'yes' in his thoughts, will be able to say 'no' when it comes to action."[128] And he adds: "Day-dreaming, reveries, memories, and anticipations, should be carefully controlled."[129]

Mortification ensures that we have the right dispositions to converse with God. Without sacrifice, it is hard to converse with the veiled God in an intimate manner, or to have a calm and happy awareness of His presence. St. Josemaría affirms,

---

[125] *The Forge*, no. 783.
[126] *The Way*, no. 196.
[127] Ibid., no. 126.
[128] Eugene Boyland, *The Spiritual Life of the Priest*, 83.
[129] Ibid., 83.

"Unless you mortify yourself, you'll never be a prayerful soul."[130]

We should not allow distractions to harm our conversation with God. Some are unavoidable, it is part of being human, but others can and ought to be driven away by practicing inner mortification.

This means that we are to be in command of our imagination, which is a great gift from God, but also a liability, if not kept under control. St. Theresa of Jesus called it "the mad woman of the house," for it can build up many images in our minds that distract us from the truly real and important things. Without guarding it, we could be living in a world of fantasy, perhaps in an attempt to escape reality, and, as a result, become open to a host of temptations.

A similar thing happens with our memory. It is, certainly, another valuable gift. If not checked, however, it could transport us deep into the past, foster nostalgic remembrances, useless regrets or grudges, and arouse fresh temptations. The founder of Opus Dei writes, "Don't think any more about your fall. Besides overwhelming and crushing you under its weight, that recollection may easily be an occasion of future temptation."[131]

An area very rich in opportunities to practice mortification is the **work** in which we are engaged. In our profession or trade, in any honest occupation, we can offer our Lord many acts of self-giving by working well, with human proficiency, punctually, and in an orderly manner, all done with desires of perfection not for human glory, but for God's glory.

---

[130] *The Way*, no. 172.
[131] Ibid., no. 262.

Study

*A*mong the good habits that characterize a "modern apostle," is a penchant for study. It shows an eagerness and seriousness in learning. St. Josemaría Escrivá puts it this way: "If you are to serve God with your mind, to study is a grave obligation for you."[132] And he added: "Study—any professional development—is a serious obligation for us."[133]

For students, to study is a duty of justice. It is due to oneself, to society, to the parents and to the teachers. To oneself, studying consists in acquiring knowledge and some skills in an orderly way, to be able to find in the future the right work to earn a living and support a family. To society, studying is a way of preparing oneself to help others by striving to advance the common good of the society in which one lives. To the parents, studying hard is a way of trying—only trying—to repay what they have done for their children. To the teachers, for they are to devote much time imparting their knowledge to the students.

In addition, study helps everyone to acquire personal maturity. The effort to study seriously one day after another, whether liking to do it or not, whether enjoying what is being studied or not, contributes to the development of such virtues as self-mastery, diligence, patience, and order.

---

[132] Ibid., no. 336.
[133] Ibid., no. 334.

The founder of Opus Dei clearly saw the importance of study for character building when he wrote,
"Student: form in yourself a solid and active piety;
be outstanding in study; have strong desires for
professional apostolate. And with that vigor in your
religious and scientific training, I promise you rapid
and far-reaching developments."[134]

He added: "Work! When you are engrossed in
professional work, the life of your soul will improve,
and you'll become more of a man for you'll get rid of
that 'carping spirit' that consumes you."[135]

More importantly, study is a means of sanctification, for it can be a way of uniting ourselves to
the veiled God. It can become a form of prayer: "An
hour of study, for a modern apostle, is an hour of
prayer."[136]

In order to elevate our study to the supernatural
level, we should invoke the Holy Spirit and offer it
to Him so that it can be presented to Him. However,
it has to be done to the best of our ability. We should
not dare to offer to God a job poorly done, a sloppy
task that would make people laugh.

We have to work with **constancy**, avoiding
butterflying from one occupation to another, sticking
to a well-thought-out schedule day after day; with
order, keeping faithfully the right priorities, beginning and ending on time, and avoiding the practice
of *cramming* before the tests. And, finally, we are to
study with **intensity**. Concentration works wonders.
We are to avoid dissipation and distractions. It is not
a matter of skimming over things, but to go deeper

---

[134] Ibid., no. 346.
[135] Ibid., no. 343.
[136] Ibid., no. 335.

into the material. *"Non multa, sed multum,"* not many things, but well,[137] advises the author of *The Way*.

It will help to tell our sheltered Father that we dedicate our study to Him for some intention: for the Church, for a friend who needs help. And while studying, we could renew this dedication a number of times. "Then, how valuable your hour of work becomes as you persevere with the same effort a little longer, a few minutes more, until the job is finished."[138] In this way, our study—and we should love studying, even after graduation, adopting the attitude of a "perpetual student"—will be a means to sanctify this noble occupation and to strive for personal sanctification.

Furthermore, it will also be a sterling means to bring others closer to God, in short, to save and to sanctify others.

St. Josemaría referred to this apostolate when he wrote: "Come follow Me, and I will make you fishers of men." Not without reason does Our Lord use these words: men—like fish—have to be caught by the head. What an evangelical depth there is in the intellectual apostolate!"[139]

Working side by side with other colleagues affords us an opportunity to draw them to the apostolate. Well-earned professional respect and prestige provides bait, an attraction, for the *fishers of men*.

We ought to hunger for knowledge, not to impress people, but rather, to put, as much as we can, all learning at the feet of Christ.

----

[137] Ibid., no. 333.
[138] *Friends of God*, no. 67.
[139] *The Way*, no. 978.

Order

This is another important virtue that ensures that we keep our priorities: *First things first!* It prevents us from deserving the classic warning of St. Augustine: "You run well, but out of the track! You will be disqualified!" Furthermore, it multiplies our time.

St. Augustine describes order as an arrangement "of equal and unequal things, giving to each its proper place."[140]

There is an observable order in nature. The entire creation is ordained to the glory of God; but man, in order to achieve his end, has to ordain himself utilizing the freedom God has given him. Since this is not done in a single act but in a multitude of actions, he has to arrange these actions among themselves, having the end in view. Hence, for man to observe order is a duty.

Accordingly, when man fails to keep this order in relation to God, he sins. The greatest disorder, in fact, is to prefer a limited creature than the infinite Creator.

So that a good action of ours would be pleasant to God, it must be ordained to its natural and supernatural goal. In this, the virtue of prudence has an essential role to play. It ordains the means to their end, and ultimately, to the fulfillment of God's plan.

----

[140] St. Augustine, *De Civitate Dei*, Bk. 19, Ch. 13.

It is the virtue of order that leads us to reach our ultimate goal—to fulfill God's will. Anything opposed to it is disorder.

In addition, order brings peace and serenity to our lives. Not in vain, St. Augustine calls peace "the tranquility of order."[141] Conversely, where there is disorder, there is anxiety.

Order should show itself in our ideas, in our mind. Not all our thoughts have the same importance. There ought to be a hierarchy and coordination among our ideas, and all of them are to be related to the supreme idea of God.

Thus, for instance, the truths of our faith, as taught by the Church, are to occupy the highest place in the order of our ideas. Then come the scientific, professional, and experimental truths, and finally, at the last place, those that are simple opinions.

Order should also reign in our love and in our affections. This means that the love for God should always occupy the number one position in our hierarchy of values, then, our love for our family both supernatural and natural, our friends and colleagues, our fellow Catholics, our fellow Christians, all our compatriots, all human beings, all creatures, etc.

Likewise, order should be lived in our actions.

- In the fulfillment of our daily plan of life, always "placing first things first," give priority to our practices of piety. God deserves the first place in our list of things to do.
- Punctually follow our schedules at home and in the workplace.
- Get up at a set time, living the "heroic minute."

....

141 Ibid.

- Meet carefully the given deadlines and avoid putting work off for the following day.
- Inform those who have to know, when we cannot be where and when we are expected.

The virtue of order should be lived in material things, in accordance with the motto: *"A place for everything, and everything in its place."* Material order is often a reflection of the inner order in our soul.

Cheerfulness

Finally, the end product of living the virtues mentioned above is a *cheerfulness* that nothing and nobody can take away from us. The reason is because living the Christian life in its fullness, seeking the hidden Lord and finding Him,[142] always comes together with a permanent joy accompanied with a deep peace.

Cheerfulness is part of the will of God for us Christians: "Serve the Lord with gladness." But it is a joy that does not depend on the situation. St. Josemaría says,

> It is not the kind we might call physiological good spirits, the happiness of a healthy animal.
>
> You must seek something more: the supernatural happiness that comes from the abandonment of everything and the

---

[142] Cf. *The Way*, no. 666.

abandonment of yourself into the loving arms of our Father God.[143]

And also, "You are unhappy? Think: there must be an obstacle between God and me. You will seldom be wrong."[144]

When we truly love the veiled God, exercising faith and hope, we are happy. On occasion, we might even want to sing, for "To sing is proper to lovers." A life of faith, hope, and love is a great life, and it is an indicator of a deep interior contact with God. It is impossible to be truly joyful if we do not converse with God.

As St. Josemaría says,

> Cheerfulness is a necessary consequence of our divine filiation, of knowing that our Father God loves us with a love of predilection, that He holds us up and helps us and forgives us.
>
> Remember this and never forget it: even if it should seem at times that everything around you is collapsing, in fact nothing is collapsing at all, because God does not lose battles.[145]

Thus, even when confronted with huge problems, we are to realize that, as St. Paul said, "For those who love God, all things work together unto good."[146]

Thus, his insistent advice makes sense: "Live always in joy. Rejoice in the Lord always; again I

---

[143] *Friends of God*, no. 12; cf. *The Way*, no. 659.
[144] *The Way*, no. 662.
[145] *The Forge*, no. 332.
[146] Rom 8:28 (*Omnia in bonum*).

say to you, rejoice."[147] We should always look on the bright side of things. What seems most overwhelming in life is not really so dark, so unbearable. If you get down to specifics, you will not draw pessimistic conclusions. We are to get out from a negative overall view, and we must trust the Lord.

Furthermore, it is important to reject sadness, for it can easily convince us that we need some consolation, a break, a compensation which could open the door to sinful actions. A sad soul is predisposed to sin. It is important to be sincere about this matter in our examination of conscience and in our spiritual direction.

Sadness is often caused by an excessive love of self. Conversely, self-forgetfulness for the sake of God and others generates joy in us. It is a type of joy that the Lord wants us to have, and it can be earned by piety, sincerity, and self-mastery. The reason for the latter is that the sweetest victory is the victory over oneself.

As in everything else, in order to acquire the virtue of cheerfulness, we are to ask the help of Our Lady. She is invoked as the *Cause of our joy!*

Epilogue

Dear reader, we will part ways here. I have made some suggestions that were also recommendations made by St. Josemaría Escrivá, and which he himself lived with heroic alacrity. They were made taking into account the free will that the veiled God has

---

[147] Phil 4:4.

granted to all of us. In other words, these are only invitations to do all these things freely *because we want to*; because we are truly convinced that it is fitting for us to do them. It is precisely this great gift of liberty that opens the door to merit, keeps our human dignity, and supports our hope for the great prize of the vision of the concealed Examiner when the Test and the Game of this present life will be over and the covering curtain will, at last, be forever removed.

These suggestions are not meant to be followed in their totality on the very first day. Almost always, a certain period of time will be needed to incorporate them gradually into our daily habits. St. Josemaría, speaking on the advancement of spiritual life, refers to this as *"in an inclined plane."* In the attempt to make step-by-step progress, the help of a spiritual director could not be over-emphasized. It is certainly very helpful to have someone who, with prudence and in a demanding fashion, will encourage us to move forward towards the supreme goal of *falling in love with the hidden God.*

Bibliography

Abad, Javier and Eugenio Fenoy. *Children: Their Training, Formation and Education.* Manila: Sinag-tala Publishers, 1995.

Bonelli, Raphael. *Palabra.* Madrid: Ediciones Palabra, July 2012.

Boyland, Eugene. *The Spiritual Life of a Priest.* Maryland: The Newman Press, 1961.

de Prada, Andres Vazquez. *The Founder of Opus Dei.* Vol. 2. New York: Scepter Publishers, Inc., 2003.

Knox, Ronald. *A Retreat for Lay People.* Lagos: Criterion Publishers, 2005.

Navarro, J. Lopez. *The Joys and Travails of a Large Family.* Manila: Sinag-tala Publishers, Inc., 1975.

Ramírez, Antonio María. *Comprometerse.* Madrid: Ediciones Palabra, 2007.

Rhonheimer, Martin. *You are the Light of the World.* Manila: Sinag-tala Publishers, 2010.

Stenson, James B. *Reading: Learning To Choose.* London and New York: Scepter Publishers, 1984.

Trese, Leo. *The Faith Explained.* Manila: Sinag-tala Publishers, 2008.

Works of Saints, Popes, and Church Documents

Compendium of the Catechism of the Catholic Church. Manila: Episcopal Commission on Catechesis and Catholic Education, 2007.

Escrivá, Josemaría. *Christ is Passing By*. Manila: Sinag-tala Publishers, 1973, 2000.

———. *Conversations with Monsignor Escrivá de Balaguer*. Manila: Sinag-tala Publishers, 1985.

———. *The Forge*. Manila: Sinag-tala Publishers, 2000.

———. *Friends of God*. Manila: Sinag-tala Publishers, 2000.

———. *Furrow*. Manila: Sinag-tala Publishers, 2000.

———. *Holy Rosary*. Manila: Sinag-tala Publishers, 2000.

———. *The Way*. Manila: Sinag-tala Publishers, 1985.

———. *The Way of the Cross*. London and New York: Scepter, 1982.

Pope Benedict XVI. *Jesus of Nazareth*. New York: Doubleday, 2007.

Pope St. John XXIII. Encyclical on the Rosary *Grata Recordatio*. September 26, 1959.

Pope St. John Paul II. *Prayer for Priests on Holy Thursday*. March 25, 1982.

Pope Paul VI. *Discourse*. October 10, 1964.

———. Pastoral Constitution *Gaudium et Spes*. December 7, 1965.

Pope Pius XII. Encyclical *Ad Apostolorum Principis*. June 29, 1958.

Sacred Congregation of Divine Worship. *Immensae Caritatis*. January 29, 1973.

St. Augustine. *Confessions*. New York: Book-of-the-Month Club, 1996; New York: Image Books, 1960.

———. *De Civitate Dei* (The City of God).

St. Leonard of Port Maurice. *The Hidden Treasure of the Holy Mass.* Rockford, Illinois: TAN Books and Publishers, Inc., 1952.

St. Teresa of Jesus. *The Life of Teresa of Jesus: The Autobiography of St. Teresa of Avila.* New York: Doubleday, Image Book, 1960.

About the Author

Born in Vic (Barcelona), Spain, in 1932, John C. Portavella obtained a Master's degree in chemistry at the University of Barcelona, Spain. In 1958, he earned a Doctorate in Canon Law from the University of Santo Tomas (Angelicum) in Rome and was ordained priest in 1959 for the Opus Dei prelature. He was then asked by the founder, St. Josemaría Escrivá, to exercise ministry in the United States and help in the apostolic work in that country. He remained in the U.S.A. until 1967, when the founder asked him to serve in the Philippines.

Portavella exercised his ministry in Cebu City, Philippines, where, in addition to imparting courses on "Theology for Lay People," he taught medical ethics at the Cebu Doctors' University, College of Medicine. From 1991 to 2011, he served in Iloilo City as spiritual director of lay men and women of different walks of life, as well as of secular priests and seminarians. For many years, he was assistant chaplain at the Westbridge School for Boys. At the same time, he taught Philosophy of Nature and Metaphysics at the St. Vincent Ferrer College Seminary, in Jaro, Iloilo, for five years.

He is currently doing pastoral work at the University of Asia and the Pacific, in Pasig City, Metro Manila.

Index

Guardian Angel, 17, 18, 20, 28,
51, 73, 74

H

Hail Holy Queen, 79
Hail Mary, 54, 71, 79, 81
Holy Communion, 38, 41, 42,
43, 53, 66, 76, 79
Holy Mass, 19, 32, 33, 37-44,
46, 53, 73, 76, 79,
see also: Eucharistic
Sacrifice
Holy purity, see: Purity
Holy Rosary, 56, 59-63, 79-80
Holy Spirit, 2, 11, 26, 28, 29,
32, 34, 37, 38, 41, 61,
64, 69, 75, 80, 81, 85,
91, 92, 103
Holy water, 71
Hope, 18, 20, 26, 39, 45, 48,
77, 78, 95, 108
Human nature, 32, 46
Humility, 8, 21, 36, 41, 48, 54,
76, 86, 91

I

Imagination, 23, 33, 89, 101
Immaculate Heart, 79-80
Incarnation, 50

J

Jesus, 1-3, 7-8, 15, 18, 21, 24,
27-29, 31-34, 37-40, 42,
47, 50, 54, 62, 67, 70-71,
74-77, 81-83, 90-91,
93-94, 96-98, 101, see
also: Christ
Jesus as Friend, 67
Job, 46
John XXIII, St. Pope, 63, 79
John Paul II, St. Pope, 40
Josemaria Escriva, St., 2-3, 5-8,
11, 13, 15-16, 18-19,
21-24, 27, 40-41, 47,
51-54, 60-62, 64-73,
75-77, 81, 83-84, 86,
89-91, 93, 95-98, 100,
102, 104, 108-109
Joseph, St., 17, 20, 28, 47, 74,
75
Justice, 48

K

Knox, Ronald, 43

L

Laziness, 15, 36, 47
Leonard of Port Maurice, St.,
39-40
Lucia of Fatima, 61, 79
Luke, St., 82

Purity, 54, 71, 76

ℛ

Recollection, 18, 87, 101
Recreation, 14
Redemption, 46, 50
Regina Coeli, 49, 50
Resolution(s), 22, 27, 28, 50,
     70, 71, 80, 88, 93
Rest, 5, 7, 14, 71, 73
Resurrection, 38, 49, 80
Retreat, 43, 88
Rosary, see: Holy Rosary

S

Sacrament of Reconciliation,
     71, 81-83, see also:
     Confession
Sacred Scripture, 62, 82,
Sacrifice(s), 11, 14, 17, 32,
     37-38, 40-44, 69, 76,
     97-98, 100
Sadness, 36, 109
Saint(s), 8, 9, 11, 17, 22, 37,
     47, 54, 65, 72, 76, 81
Sanctification, 47, 66, 81, 82,
     85, 103, 104
Sanctifying grace, 81
Satan, 15, 71, 74
Scripture, see: Sacred
     Scripture
Self-mastery, 102, 109

Sign of the Cross, 71, 80
Sincerity, 86, 109
Sin(s), 16, 18, 20-22, 24,
     38-39, 43, 49, 71, 75,
     80-84, 94-98, 105, 109
Sorrow of love, 70
Sorrow of pride, 70
Soul(s), 7, 14, 19, 23, 26, 33,
     41, 43, 44, 49, 64, 69,
     74, 81, 82, 84, 85, 86,
     96, 97, 99, 101, 103,
     107, 109
Souls in Purgatory, 17, 22,
     72-73
Spiritual Communion(s), 54,
     76
Spiritual direction, 60, 85, 86,
     109
Spiritual director, 3, 7, 65, 85,
     86, 110
Spiritual reading, 64-69
Study, 9, 102-104
Suffering(s), 97-99

𝔗

Tabernacle, the, 25, 34, 53-54,
     87
Te Deum, 81
Temperance, 48, 100
Temptation(s), 18, 27, 82, 86,
     99, 101
Teresa, St., 33, 71

About Leonine Publishers

Leonine Publishers LLC makes fine Catholic literature available to Catholics throughout the English-speaking world. Leonine Publishers offers an innovative "hybrid" approach to book publication that helps authors as well as readers. Please visit our web site at www.leoninepublishers.com to learn more about us. Browse our online bookstore to find more solid Catholic titles to uplift, challenge, and inspire.

Our patron and namesake is Pope Leo XIII, a prudent, yet uncompromising pope during the stormy years at the close of the 19th century. Please join us as we ask his intercession for our family of readers and authors.

Do you have a book inside you? Visit our web site today. Leonine Publishers accepts manuscripts from Catholic authors like you. If your book is selected for publication, you will have an active part in the production process. This book is an example of our growing selection of literature for the busy Catholic reader of the 21st century.

www.leoninepublishers.com

CPSIA information can be obtained
at www.ICGtesting.com
Printed in the USA
BVOW09s0446041117
499542BV00002B/372/P